Indian Country

AMERICAN INDIAN STUDIES SERIES

Bawaajimo: A Dialect of Dreams in Anishinaabe Language and Literature, Margaret Noodin | 978-1-61186-105-1

Centering Anishinaabeg Studies: Understanding the World through Stories, edited by Jill Doerfler, Niigaanwewidam James Sinclair, and Heidi Kiiwetinepinesiik Stark | 978-1-61186-067-2

Curator of Ephemera at the New Museum for Archaic Media, Heid E. Erdrich | 978-1-61186-246-1

Document of Expectations, Devon Abbott Mihesuah | 978-1-61186-011-5

Dragonfly Dance, Denise K. Lajimodiere | 978-0-87013-982-6

Facing the Future: The Indian Child Welfare Act at 30, edited by Matthew L. M. Fletcher, Wenona T. Singel, and Kathryn E. Fort | 978-0-87013-860-7

Follow the Blackbirds, Gwen Nell Westerman | 978-1-61186-092-4

Indian Country: Telling a Story in a Digital Age, Victoria L. LaPoe and Benjamin Rex LaPoe II | 978-1-61186-226-3

The Indian Who Bombed Berlin and Other Stories, Ralph Salisbury | 978-0-87013-847-8

Masculindians: Conversations about Indigenous Manhood, edited by Sam McKegney | 978-1-61186-129-7

Mediating Indianness, edited by Cathy Covell Waegner | 978-1-61186-151-8

The Murder of Joe White: Ojibwe Leadership and Colonialism in Wisconsin, Erik M. Redix | 978-1-61186-145-7

National Monuments, Heid E. Erdrich | 978-0-87013-848-5

Ogimawkwe Mitigwaki (Queen of the Woods), Simon Pokagon | 978-0-87013-987-1

Ottawa Stories from the Springs: anishinaabe dibaadjimowinan wodi gaa binjibaamigak wodi mookodjiwong e zhinikaadek, translated and edited by Howard Webkamigad | 978-1-61186-137-2

Plain of Jars and Other Stories, Geary Hobson | 978-0-87013-998-7

Sacred Wilderness, Susan Power | 978-1-61186-111-2

Seeing Red—Hollywood's Pixeled Skins: American Indians and Film, edited by LeAnne Howe, Harvey Markowitz, and Denise K. Cummings | 978-1-61186-081-8

Shedding Skins: Four Sioux Poets, edited by Adrian C. Louis | 978-0-87013-823-2

Sounding Thunder: The Stories of Francis Pegahmagabow, Brian D. McInnes | 978-1-61186-225-6

Stories for a Lost Child, Carter Meland | 978-1-61186-244-7

Stories through Theories/Theories through Stories: North American Indian Writing, Storytelling, and Critique, edited by Gordon D. Henry Jr., Nieves Pascual Soler, and Silvia Martinez-Falquina | 978-0-87013-841-6

That Guy Wolf Dancing, Elizabeth Cook-Lynn | 978-1-61186-138-9

Those Who Belong: Identity, Family, Blood, and Citizenship among the White Earth Anishinaabeg, Jill Doerfler | 978-1-61186-169-3

Visualities: Perspectives on Contemporary American Indian Film and Art, edited by Denise K. Cummings | 978-0-87013-999-4

Writing Home: Indigenous Narratives of Resistance, Michael D. Wilson | 978-0-87013-818-8

Indian Country

TELLING A STORY IN A DIGITAL AGE

Victoria L. LaPoe and Benjamin Rex LaPoe II

MICHIGAN STATE UNIVERSITY PRESS • *East Lansing*

All royalties for this book are generously donated by the authors
to the Native American Journalists Fellowship program.

The paper used in this publication meets the minimum requirements of
ANSI/NISO Z39.48-1992 (R 1997) (Permanence of Paper).

Michigan State University Press
East Lansing, Michigan 48823-5245

Printed and bound in the United States of America.

25 24 23 22 21 20 19 18 17   1 2 3 4 5 6 7 8 9 10

LIBRARY OF CONGRESS CATALOGING-IN-PUBLICATION DATA
Names: LaPoe, Victoria, 1977– author. | LaPoe, Benjamin Rex, author.
Title: Indian country : telling a story in a digital age / Victoria L. LaPoe and Benjamin Rex LaPoe II.
Description: East Lansing : Michigan State University Press, [2017] | Series: American Indian studies series
| Includes bibliographical references and index.
Identifiers: LCCN 2016027173| ISBN 9781611862263 (pbk. : alk. paper) | ISBN 9781609175115 (pdf)
| ISBN 9781628952827 (epub) | ISBN 9781628962826 (kindle)
Subjects: LCSH: Indian newspapers. | Indian mass media. | Mass media—Technological innovations.
Classification: LCC PN4883 .L53 2017 | DDC 071.3089/97—dc23 LC record available
at https://lccn.loc.gov/2016027173

Book design by Charlie Sharp, Sharp Des!gns, East Lansing, Michigan
Cover design by Ron DeMarse
Cover image is *Medicine Wheel Earth* ©2016 by Elizabeth DeMarse
and is used with permission. All rights reserved.

Michigan State University Press is a member of the Green Press Initiative and is committed to developing
and encouraging ecologically responsible publishing practices. For more information about the Green
Press Initiative and the use of recycled paper in book publishing, please visit *www.greenpressinitiative.org*.

Visit Michigan State University Press at *www.msupress.org*.

Contents

Preface

This research explores how digital media are changing the rich cultural act of storytelling within Native communities. The norms and routines of the non-Native press often leave consumers with a stereotypical view of American Indians.

Change is a pivotal component to this research, underway now for four years. Marley Shebala was one of the biggest changes since the interviews for this research began. Marley is no longer at the *Navajo Times*. She went on to start a website and professional journal called "Marley Shebala's Notebook." She notes on her site that it is part of the Dine' Resources & Information Center, and its goal is to "keep an eye on the Navajo government." She also works for the *Gallup Independent* in New Mexico. Noel Lyn Smith, also a former *Navajo Times* reporter, is now a reporter for the Farmington *Daily Times* in New Mexico. She has been quoted often and generously by the Huffington Post on topics such as politics at the Navajo Nation. You haven't even had a chance to read the beginning of this book yet, but as you see this industry changes. The industry changes whether covering stories in Indian Country or any other place, but readers have to start somewhere to understand the power of the story and how it may or may not be changing with digital media. What better place to look than in Indian Country with people who have honored the story for hundreds of years?

Acknowledgments

We would specifically like to thank all of the Native journalists and Native communities who were willing to invite Victoria in their homes and lives to understand how digital media may be affecting the American Indian communities. A very large thank you to Joaqlin Estus of KNBA in Anchorage, Alaska, who looked at multiple versions of this text. She was beyond helpful and even gave ideas to further the research in this area. Also a special thank you to journalist, blogger, and historian Mark Trahant, who was always just a Facebook message away if I had any questions.

A special thank you to Dr. Andrea Miller and Dr. Ralph Izard. Dr. Miller supported this research from its inception and even through the birth of a child. There is not a word that is detailed enough in the English language to express gratitude for her support. We must extend a great amount of appreciation to Dr. Ralph Izard, executive director of the Media Diversity Forum, who has been an advocate for diversity and a champion supporter of Native research.

Thank you to Dr. Larry and Susan Patrick of Patrick Communications for financial support of this project.

A special thank you to our son, Dominic, who was up with us many nights as we wrote this research. We must also thank the man who taught us about Native culture and the importance of each person, tribe, and community and its connection to all things, Victoria's grandfather, William. Wado!

Any and all authors' proceeds have been set up to be routed directly to the Native American Journalists Association to help support the future stories and storytellers of Indian Country. The stories within this book are not for profit, but instead to enrich understanding of history—a circle of those who have served as elders within our journalism community to the next generation.

Introduction

Storytelling is very important still to Native communities and the fact that Native stories aren't told by the mainstream media. You know, if we don't tell them who will?

—Peggy Berryhill, President/General Manager, KGUA

Storytelling is a key part of American Indian culture, ritualistically passed-down history from one generation to the next.[1] Stories in Indian Country are often *oral* and rich in detail and language. Breadth and depth are important when telling Native stories as, historically, American Indian stories served as a form of recording history.[2]

Stories become a part of everyday Native life, included in music, dances, festivals, medicine, and art. Each story has a reason—history, moral tale, and even a community's place in society. Each American Indian tribe is unique, with its own history and therefore with its own stories. Some storytellers argue that the stories themselves are living artifacts, just one generation from being extinct if not spread by word of mouth any longer.[3]

Digital media, which include the entire scope of the Internet, social media, and mobile applications, allow for the extension of this storytelling. The Native community now has opportunities to create and discuss content online on both Native and non-Native platforms. Native issues are making their way to the mainstream media as digital platforms are evolving. Native people also do not have to solely rely on non-Native people for inclusion in history or news coverage. However, to gain understanding of how Native journalists are extending their stories and coverage through digital platforms, I chose to evaluate Native newsroom norms and routines.

Stories are the heart and soul of the journalism profession, and journalists want to publish the most newsworthy, revenue-generating news.[4] Because of this, American Indian stories get little to no media attention unless they are groundbreaking, as in the case of Chester Nez, the last original Navajo code talker who passed away in June 2014. Therefore, oral storytelling is imperative to share perspectives and record history.[5] While the number of American Indian journalists has grown of late,[6] this group is still underrepresented in non-Native newsrooms, with most Native journalists working within tribal media. Some Native scholars and professionals argue that most American Indians do not even consider journalism a career choice because of entry barriers such as language, culture, and education.[7] It was our experience during this research that this may not be the case.

American Indian and minority organizations provided an outpouring of support for this study, enthused that a Native person was conducting Native research. Victoria LaPoe interviewed and observed key storytellers identified within Indian Country by Native and minority organizations such as the Native American Journalists Association (NAJA) and the Minorities and Communication division of the Association for Education in Journalism and Mass Communication. The interviews included visiting multiple Native news organizations to observe the use of digital media within daily news coverage routines.

Growth of Native Visibility in the Digital Age

"American Indians are often described as the most invisible minority."[8] The Native community is so invisible that American Indians are often placed in research's "other" category, making it hard to specifically extract information on Native issues. In a 2015 Pew Research Center survey examining race and social media, the study included those who are white, black, and Latino.[9] I displayed these numbers in a digital storytelling class, and one student from Africa said if you do this type of work, please have a place for me in this study—meaning he did not identify as "black." The point of this story is that like this student who spoke up in my large digital storytelling lecture, there has not been a place for American Indians in studies. When examining polls and studies, often American Indians are forgotten or not included because we are considered a minority of minorities.

With the invisibility of Native people among the masses, the most common way non-Natives learn about Native culture is through mass media, and, unfortunately, mass media often focus on stereotypical images.[10] The schemas these stereotypes fortify are not only offensive but culturally insidious and harmful to uninformed audiences. For example, during Oklahoma State's 2014 opening home game against Florida State, a group of students displayed a racially insensitive sign that read "SEND 'EM HOME #TRAIL_OF_TEARS #GOPOKES." A picture of this sign almost instantly went viral and sparked outrage and hurt across the Internet. Supposedly not realizing the sign was offensive, Austin Buchanan, the student who created the sign, issued an apology on behalf of those involved in the making and displaying of the sign. In the digital age, cultural ignorance permeates every aspect of society but hits minorities the hardest. American Indian culture is greatly marginalized when Natives are displayed as being part of the "other" or as non-Natives "playing Indian." Media encourage such ideas when they depict American Indians as not exactly like the reader, instead distant and exotic, creating a vicious cycle of isolationism.[11]

While on social media there was support in Indian Country for the 2015 movie *The Revenant*, not all Native people agreed it was a move forward when it came to images of Native people. Peggy Berryhill, general manager of KGUA radio, said that the wife in the movie still spoke in a stereotypical Hollywood "whispering" voice and that Native people are shown as "stoic" rather than as a community with depth and range. She said that not until movies with Native directors are seen as the mainstream and not "ethnic" does she see Hollywood portraying a more accurate view of Indian Country. She noted that within the film industry there was "equality in the sense because we [Native people] have festival circuits, but not equity because we are seen as ethnic media."[12] She stated that she did not want to come across as saying Native people need acceptance from the mainstream, but instead to stress that for Native women and others to be represented with range, changes needed to be made within the film industry. Meanwhile in an article at Indian Country Today Media Network, a lead actor in the film said that it had cultural advisors to attempt to avoid stereotypes.[13]

Some media personalities are aiming to change this trend of showcasing Native people in a stereotypical fashion. For example, in a satirical video targeting FedEx's hypocritical sponsorship of the Washington Redskins, artist/filmmaker Paul Judd pokes fun at the company by saying they "embrace racism" by supporting the racist team name.[14] The video ends with a link leading to a petition urging Redskins owner Dan Snyder to discontinue use of the name as well as several hashtags viewers can use on Twitter to raise awareness to this issue. In July 2014, CBS announced it would let its employees decide if they wanted to use the offensive name while reporting. ESPN followed suit that August. Tony Dungy and Phil Simms, two prominent NFL analysts who work for NBC and CBS, respectively, promised to discontinue their personal use of the name starting in the 2014 NFL season.[15]

Advocate, writer, lecturer, Presidential Medal of Freedom recipient, and president and executive director of the Morning Star Institute, an organization that supports advocacy for Native Peoples' tradition and culture, Suzan Harjo has fought against the offensive Washington name since the 1960s.[16] Fitting for this digital storytelling project, Harjo answered in several messages from her BlackBerry. She wrote that she first learned about the issues surrounding the Washington name conflict in 1962 from Clyde Warrior, Ponca, who founded the National Indian Youth Council. The council was one of the main groups that got rid of the first "Indian" mascot to fall in American sports, "Little Red" at the University of Oklahoma. Harjo believes Native coverage begins from a starting point of knowing that the overwhelming majority of Native people want an end to the disparaging name of the Washington franchise. Non-Native media often start by asking what Native people think but all too often are distracted by the few Native people the franchise promotes most through the exchange of money), even suggesting equivalence between their handful and all major national Native organizations and their members and constituents. In terms of the Washington NFL name conflict, she says social media efforts are most effective in terms of rallying and informing the base. Those who want change are doing well, but so are those who don't. In her eyes, social media have made rapid responses and instantly sharing information possible.[17]

In spite of skewed stereotypes, the Native population is not nearly as far detached from society and the masses as the mainstream lack of coverage leads the public to believe. The United States contains 566 federally recognized tribes.[18] According to the 2010 U.S. census of American Indians and Alaska Natives, the population grew by 1.5 percent from the previous census, totaling 6.3 million people.[19] The U.S. Census projects that by 2060, the Native population number will grow to more than 10 million American Indians and Alaska Natives. From 2004–14, American Indians and Alaska Natives have increased by nearly 27 percent. When breaking down Native populations in the United States, the following states have more than 100,000 American Indians and Alaska Natives; these include California, Oklahoma, Arizona, Texas, New York, New Mexico, Washington, North Carolina, Florida, Michigan, Alaska, Oregon, Colorado, Pennsylvania, and Minnesota. Twenty-two percent of American Indians and Alaska Natives live on or in a combination of Indian areas or Alaska Native villages, and nearly 29 percent of Native Americans live in poverty, compared to 15 percent for the overall United States. The median income for Native families is around $35,000 in comparison with $50,000 for the overall United States.[20]

In comparison to other communities, the Native population may seem small, but digital media are imperative to minority groups and allow them to have a salient voice. For example, American Indians had a particular interest in the 2012 reelection of President Barack Obama. Support for the president grew after his 2008 election because Native people started seeing a growth in federal trust and improved tribal gaming relationships.[21]

During the 2012 presidential election, the NAJA constantly updated social media sites. On Facebook and Twitter, members and followers received overall election numbers and information on Natives reelected across the country.[22] The day after the 2012 presidential election, the *Navajo Times* reported Navajos assisted in President Obama's reelection while increasing public attention on issues pertinent to Native communities. In two counties, the vote was 2–1 for President Obama.[23] The overall social media outcome: Natives increased their visibility by increasing Native voter news coverage within social media.

With the expansion of Native information and images also comes the opportunity for Natives to respond. Leading up to Thanksgiving 2012, headlines such as this one appeared on CNN: "White Girls Play Indian."[24] The article displayed a Victoria's Secret supermodel in a full-length mock-feather headdress, turquoise jewelry, and a scant leopard-print bikini for the company's December 4, 2012, holiday fashion show. The show turned out to be the highest-rated program of the night across the networks with 9.3 million viewers.[25] Prior to this incident, the music group No Doubt also released a music video for "Looking Hot" that contained stereotypical images such as teepees. Both groups apologized, and the incident led to coverage such as the CNN article on people "playing Indian" for profit. While the Internet allowed for the "White Girls Play Indian" story to circulate quickly and receive unfavorable responses from Native organizations, websites also brought to light the clear lack of understanding of the Native community. Comments under CNN's story illustrated this misunderstanding by non-Native readers:

> Native Americans shouldn't be so sensitive. What's so sacred about how they dress or a sexy woman in a skimpy Indian outfit?? If it offends your delicate sensitivities . . . get over it.
>
> You certainly have no problem taking advantage of our capitalist culture and tax benefits. . . . I know Europeans screwed you over BIG time, but wearing one of your symbols is not inherently a disrespectful thing.

While the Internet enables more information and image circulation as well as response and discussion of inappropriate images and narratives, society still needs an education in debunking old views and myths about Native culture. Stereotypical, false images of American Indians demean this culture and ignore the suffering endured—suffering that is a part of American Indian history.[26] Scholars note that American Indians have suffered much like African Americans because both groups have endured slavery and stripping of not only land, but language and even families.[27]

Including the Native Community as a Part of Norms and Routines

For non-Native media to move toward more inclusivity and away from the stereotypes, journalists need awareness of the Native community.[28] Non-Natives must understand each tribe is unique. Non-Native media can dramatically change if they become inclusive with American Indian coverage from multiple Native perspectives.[29] Journalists and scholars alike argue that mainstream media need to consider a holistic approach toward marginalized groups. For example, mainstream media should avoid covering minority groups only in negative situations to avoid creating narrow stereotypes. Non-Native newsrooms instead should view the American Indian community as a beat, visiting and following-up with the Native communities they are covering.[30] By keeping up to date with a constantly evolving population, the media can help diminish harmful stereotypes and therefore empower the Native communities crippled by them.

Content Control

Another issue facing Native news outlets is who controls the media. In non-Native news, advertisers, corporate ownership, government officials, and even consumers vie for content management.[31] Tribes often are like media ownership groups; the content on tribal sites depends on what the tribe allows for publication—essentially censorship of content.[32]

Research on the norms and routines of Native media is nonexistent, but these rituals are tied closely to the gatekeeping of news, where the media have a patterned way of covering and producing news content through beat, sourcing, and/or other forms of news coverage.[33] In general, most Native news organizations are advocates of civic, also defined as community, journalism, providing information from and about the community—similar to how many mainstream local news outlets view their roles. Tribally independent Native media report on the tribal government to keep public officials in check and citizens informed, but tribal councils have shut down Native news organizations for questioning authority.[34] In the 1980s, the Navajo tribal council closed the *Navajo Times* during what Navajo people still refer to today as a civil war.[35] Months after this riot, the paper reopened and is now a free and separate press from the tribe.[36]

Some Natives have started their own news outlets because of their frustration with the editing of their work on Native sites.

> I was writing for *Indian Country Today*. I did write for them—they had published a few of my articles. They would limit my word count. They would edit my stuff. So, I just wanted to get away from this. . . . I had the idea doing of doing a bigger scale thing.[37]

In 2000, the Cherokee Nation passed an Independent Press Act in efforts to stop censorship, which allowed for a separation between the Nation and the editorial function of the *Cherokee Phoenix*. The tribe still funds the paper, but no branch of government can try to censor the news.

> In fact, we have had several papers that have come to me to talk about our press act and to find ways to implement something similar with their tribe. The Osage Nation has an independent press act that is modeled after ours. The Eastern Band of Cherokee Indians has a press act modeled after ours, and there's a couple of other

tribes that have done that as well. Just a couple months ago, I spoke to a tribe in California, and they are looking to do the same thing. It is starting to slowly catch on in Indian Country, and I'm hoping it continues to move in this direction.[38]

Growth of Native and Diverse Media

While some news audiences are declining, diverse media users have grown in news consumption, including digitally.[39] In a survey conducted by New American Media in 2009, diverse media increased their reach by 16 percent over four years. This reach included fifty-seven million African Americans, Latinos, and Asian Americans. Media growth included overall diverse radio stations and specifically Asian American television, with growth by 30 percent.[40]

Diverse media consumers expose a different angle in their news versus mainstream news coverage. Diverse media focus more on the effects to the minority audience, cover issues and events connected to people of color, and support understanding a multicultural world.[41] Diverse media have a different news coverage role than the overall mainstream media. This media are mostly small- to medium-market-sized and are dependent on advertising from small businesses, which means fewer resources compared to mainstream media with large investors. Traditionally, diverse media reflect roles of advocacy, community, and international/multicultural perspective.[42]

Diverse media also give visibility to groups that often are invisible in the mainstream press.[43] These media are often local or regional and allow for coverage of events the mainstream press may not cover. For example, during the week of September 18, 2014, the American Indian community took a heavy historical blow when four Navajo code talkers died in the span of a week. After Googling key terms such as "code talker death" or "four code talkers die," no recent relevant articles appeared even though the *Navajo Times* published an article about them. If a news consumer can't access this kind of information when he or she actively searches for it using the world's most prevalent search engine, how can an average news consumer who only scans headlines from national news outlets ever expect to know about it? While social media groups stress community by providing opportunities for individuals to build on conversation through posts, diverse media began stressing the collectiveness of the overall Native community and group long before Facebook.[44]

The *Cherokee Phoenix* serves as an example of growing online media. The *Cherokee Phoenix* is the oldest American Indian newspaper on record and still publishes in its traditional form in addition to an electronic newsletter, on the web, and by smartphone application.[45] The paper originated in the 1800s to spread news from one Cherokee region to another until the state of Georgia, with the support of the United States government, forced this nation to disperse and eventually for southeastern tribes to relocate in what is identified as the Trail of Tears.[46]

Two hundred years after the American Indian Removal Act of the 1830s, American Indians can find out the latest in news and sports as well as listen to Cherokee radio and read the original Cherokee Nation language, ᏣᎳᎩ.

> Overall our audience is definitely growing. I think that with all the different products we have available, the number of people we can potentially reach is so much greater, but we want to be able to reach everyone . . . here in Cherokee Nation we still have many citizens that live in rural areas that it may not have an Internet connection, may not have a computer in their home, and some of them may not have running water so the challenge for us is finding ways to reach *every* citizen.[47]

Bryan Pollard, executive editor of the *Cherokee Phoenix*, rose in the ranks to bring the newspaper into the digital age. Hired in 2007, Pollard explained that his first initiative was to launch a website, which he did within three to four months of becoming executive editor. From there, he said, everything flowed; the mobile Cherokee newspaper app and the Facebook page all came together.

> We had the newspaper and we already knew the newspaper was very popular, that we had a very steady audience of newspaper readers, but we wanted to reach all those thousands and thousands of Cherokees that didn't read a newspaper. . . . If we are going to continue to be an important publication to Cherokee people, we of course have to retain our current audience, but we also have to reach out to our future audience, younger people who are going to continue to rely on the *Cherokee Phoenix* as they become adults and progress through life and start their own families and all those things.[48]

With infrastructure issues on reservations, some Natives skipped a step with digital media and instead moved to connecting through mobile devices. Transitioning to mobile media is not unusual and has also occurred in other countries such as

Chile where smartphone ownership is nearly at a ratio of one phone to one person. The move to mobility allowed many Native news organizations to focus on creating content for mobile applications and in training its staff in this latest technology.[49]

In 2013, Indian Country and the Associated Press (AP) renewed an interest in developing a partnership. Two years later, the AP and Indian Country do not have a direct relationship, where Native news organizations would directly feed into the AP news service; however, the AP did have a presence at the 2015 NAJA conference, attending events and meeting with up-and-coming Native journalists.[50] If this relationship is developed further with the AP, history truly could repeat itself. In the late 1800s, the first American Indian woman who owned a newspaper was a Cherokee named Myrta Eddleman. She advanced the business of her paper by contracting with the AP. As a result, her paper was able to publish developing stories outside of Indian Country and, therefore, gained nearly a thousand paid subscribers.[51] There are talks within Indian Country today to create a wire service with the AP. The service would be a sharing of tribal newspaper and Native radio news.[52]

Digital Divide and Native Communities

While the culture is rich with storytelling, Indian Country does not have equal access to technology, creating what scholars identify as a digital divide.[53] The younger Native generation has a desire for information faster than the traditional weekly and monthly publication of Native news. Meanwhile, many reservations still do not have running water or electricity much less computers.[54]

Generational and infrastructural digital barriers remain in Indian Country.[55] The Navajo Nation, for instance, has little digital access. "A lot of those folks do rely on that tribal newspaper to understand what is going on." Jeff Harjo, who is currently running for chief of the Seminole Nation of Oklahoma and was NAJA executive director at the time of his interview, said that when he visits his mother in Oklahoma, he stands on the northwest corner of her carport to gain Internet access.[56]

The Pew Research Center's Project for Excellence found that 43 percent of Natives have broadband access at home, compared to the overall national number of 60 percent. American Indians and Alaska Natives typically live in remote, rural, and isolated areas; connectivity for the nation's rural areas is 50 percent, 7 percent higher than the connectivity for the overall Native community. In comparison to others, more than 67 percent of Asian Americans, 59 percent of African Americans, and 49 percent of Latinos have broadband. Less than 10 percent of reservation and tribal lands have broadband.[57]

Overall, word of mouth, newspaper, and radio are still the most-used media in Indian Country. Both radio and TV saw growth in 2011. Meanwhile, challenges still remain for print. During 2011, a large Native paper, *Indian Country*, moved its headquarters to New York and switched to a magazine style focusing efforts online, and another, *News from Indian Country*, kept its newspaper style but concentrated on online publications.[58]

Some reservations such as the Navajo, Hopi, and Pasqua Yaqui Nations have brought fiber-optic cables to their land and are sharing wireless. The Minnesota Shakopees have a strong economic development system and generously help other tribes that have digital needs.[59] Meanwhile, California's Yurok Tribe created a "super" Wi-Fi that allows for long-distance connection.

Tribal leaders asked the Federal Communications Commission to approve the increase in broadband, wireless, and radio services in rural Indian Country.[60]

CHAPTER 1

Native Storytelling

Communication existed in America long before Christopher Columbus arrived in 1492. "Inca, Aztec, and Maya all had elaborate systems of recording, transferring, and storing records, including the work of scribes who wrote on bark tablets" and stone carvings.[1] Tribes in both the Northern and Southern Hemispheres used a complex maze of trails that spanned the continents for runners to disseminate messages and network with other tribes; Aztecs used a combination of color banners to communicate with mass audiences in highly populated areas.[2] Another common medium, an oral tradition of storytelling, was popular among the tribes for distributing and preserving knowledge. Although many ways of life changed, to put it lightly, for American Indians post–European colonization, ritualistic Native storytelling changed little—one of the few pluralistic threads that helped those communities survive. Digital media may possibly be changing the social fabric as well as norms and routines of Native storytelling. Thus, this research will use norms and routines theory to inform and guide the study's research questions.

Native Storytelling and Digital Media

Traditionally, most Native communities used storytelling as the primary instrument for historical record-keeping. While there are some similarities among American Indian communities, each American Indian and his/her tribal community has its own unique story, which is why it was essential for the individual histories to be recorded. The stories contain lessons that helped individuals and families make sense of how they and the tribe fit into the larger collective world.[3]

American Indians orally shared these *authentic* stories with their children and grandchildren—from one generation to the next. Authentic stories are defined as oral communication from people who are connected to a language through "heritage and expertise."[4] Not telling these stories threatened a key part of the community's history.

Journalism is connected to Native storytelling through the ritualistic sharing of stories within American Indian communities. Carey posits that "a ritual view of communication is directed not toward the extension of messages in space but toward the maintenance of stories in time."[5] This ritualistic view of communication aptly describes American Indian storytelling because there is a similar thread between both ritual and Native storytelling; a collective view of communication, which includes preservation of history, community, religion, and fellowship, fits both Native culture and ritual communication.[6] Digital media present variables that may change and enhance the nature of ritualistic storytelling in American Indian communities.

Scholarly research addressing Native news and digital media is extremely sparse. However, research on mainstream media and digital platforms may provide insight into how digital media may or may not advance Native storytelling. In an examination of four convergent mainstream newsrooms, newspapers that are partnerships with television and web news organizations, print journalists had concerns that the immediacy of relaying information through digital platforms would outweigh effective storytelling.[7] As expected, the print journalists noted that they went to school to produce ethical journalism—not to multitask uploading video and updating the web. Many of the journalists had a difficult time with the constant apprising of information digitally. Social media allow for the visibility of breaking news stories before the mainstream media have yet had a chance to report on them. With tragic events such as the 2012 Colorado theater shooting, which resulted in twelve people dead and fifty-eight injured, eyewitnesses turned to social media to give firsthand accounts and uploaded video on YouTube.[8] Hashtags even alerted friends and family that those they knew were killed.[9]

Through posts on Facebook and Twitter, social media users cover critical events that mainstream media chose to ignore; norms, routines, and gatekeeping are the primary contributors that determine what stories are covered.[10] In 2011, a Twitter user unknowingly broadcast the military operation killing Osama bin Laden after the user tweeted about a helicopter hovering in the middle of the night.[11] In 2009, the United States asked Twitter to delay a network upgrade so there was no downtime for Twitter users in Iran who wanted to protest the presidential election.[12] During a natural disaster in Japan, Twitter users broadcast crisis messages faster than any professional news medium; tweets about the Japanese earthquake occurred within a minute and twenty seconds.[13]

Native Connectivity and Community

American Indians with basic Internet connectivity have been able to spread their stories to millions online through social media. There are multiple Facebook and Twitter accounts tribes use to contact Native news organizations about specific Native causes. While not everyone has connectivity, the essence of the digital divide, facilities at schools and libraries help people connect and share their information.[14]

In addition to the previously mentioned media forms, American Indian websites have increased since 1994.[15] Sites include information on education, PowWows, events, language, business, and tribal and genealogy resources.[16] Within the past five years, Native news organizations have added newscasts and podcasts to their sites and mobile applications to offer users the latest news from Indian Country.[17]

While there has been an increase in Native information, a digital divide persists. Defined as "an unequal access to information technology based on income, race, ethnicity, gender, age, and geography," this divide cripples Native media and communication.[18] Compared to the rest of the United States and other minority groups, American Indians have a lower broadband penetration. "Word of mouth," print, and radio are still the overall preferred forms of communication but are somewhat outdated in a highly digital world.[19]

The digital divide specifically affects minorities and their advancement economically.[20] Scholars argue that having technology and instruction on how to effectively use it available to women and people of color would help bridge this gap. Mobility of not only minorities but also young adults, smartphone users, and other demographics is beginning to narrow the digital divide. African Americans and English-speaking Latinos are as likely as whites to own any sort of mobile phone and are more likely to use their phone for a wider range of activities.[21] With the growth of minorities in the United States and the growth of digital media, technology provides the opportunity to portray this nation in an accurate, diverse manner.[22] Providing a more honest view digitally not only affects who gets news and who is heard, but also how the world views the United States.

Norms and Routines

As Berkowitz explains, the individual journalist does not typically work alone or invent his/her own rules on how she/he covers a story.[23] What journalists consider the norm and/or routine in covering stories are embedded practices within newsroom culture. With time constraints and multiple news holes to fill, journalists do not always stray from what they do not understand or can't explain on the news deadline clock. Unfortunately, Native tribes often fall in this category, and coverage of Native people emerges only when there is a type of news frame journalists typically can understand outside of Native culture, such as conflict or crime.

To understand how the news results in its final published or aired form, scholars have studied the internal and external influences in producing news, including a journalists' routine. Shoemaker and Reese's model includes five "hierarchy of influence" levels: ideological, extramedia, organization, routine, and individual. In the center of this model is the individual journalist, influenced by all other factors. The relationship between the journalist and these factors define how he or she creates news content.[24]

Journalists learn to see in certain ways that can then be covered through work routines in order to process materials.[25] The judgment of "what is news" is considered sacred knowledge that differentiates journalists from other "common" people.[26] The mainstream media do not have the same news coverage routines as diverse focused media organizations. Most journalists in mainstream news operations have not taken the time to understand the inner workings of minority communities, explaining, in part, why stereotypical mainstream news continues.[27] Journalists are supposed to possess *news* values to be successful, but few can define these routine elements that consistently exclude minorities.[28] News workers depend on what they perceive as newsworthy, and often the "who" and "what" do not include minority audiences.[29]

Media organizations look to each other to confirm and validate decisions.[30] While journalists evaluate one another these professionals do not invite criticism from the public or outside groups.[31] Newspapers cater to their news audiences by being able to provide lengthier detailed content. Generally speaking, newspaper readers tend to be more educated compared to broadcast audiences. In contrast, local television journalists have the largest time and size constraints; these television journalists try to report stories that will fit into very short segments.[32]

Patterns of media may be compared to tribal ownership of Native media. Ownership influences the news that media consumers receive.[33] Researchers tend to shy away from the fact that news stories tend to mirror the policy preferences of media ownership groups; news organizations hire staff that fits their policy, give stories to people who will cover them the "policy-way," and edit stories in a manner to fit the policy.[34]

Some journalists undermine their job as "watchdogs" when they elevate the newsworthiness status of elite sources. Journalists, in turn, become "lapdogs"—in part because of newsroom constraints—but this influences the type of coverage news consumers receive.[35] Officials and business representatives oftentimes have greater access to news media than those with less power.[36] Diminished resources force journalists to rely on official, or "elite," sound bites more often because journalists do not have as much time to search for other sources that may have a different interpretation.[37] To some, official sources equal an accurate view of the truth.[38] Official voices essentially set the barometer for how a community should act and feel about an issue, and often those who are ignored are women and people of color.[39] For many reasons, most of these official sources tend to be disproportionately white.[40]

Journalists rely on mostly white males as sources; thus, marginal groups become invisible. The media often choose sources based on that person's position and/or authority within the community,[41] which leads consumers to view one race as dominant and the other as recessive or nonexistent.[42] Consequently, minority groups distrust mainstream media and white officials and rely instead on more personal forms of communication for information, such as community organizations and churches.[43]

Jha and Izard find that news coverage of American Indians included primarily white sources even within diverse communities.[44] These racial findings are consistent with research from Hurricane Katrina and the Deepwater Horizon disaster.[45] During Katrina, media showed visuals of whites as powerful and African Americans as negative, displaying whites as officials helping African American victims.[46] Miller and Roberts conducted an open-ended survey that asked respondents the images they remembered from Katrina and compared the responses to media images of the hurricane. The most memorable content was associated with race and gender and was the same images that media repeatedly displayed.[47]

Mainstream media have not consistently portrayed minority audiences within news stories. Historically, the mainstream media excluded minorities altogether, included minorities only when they were perceived as a threat to their "white" audiences, addressed minority groups when there was a conflict, and/or presented minorities through stereotypes.[48] Simply mentioning race can negatively impact how nonminorities feel about the individuals mentioned in news stories, providing heightened pressure on how journalists report on a story covering a diverse audience.[49] Therefore, the hope for the future is a more concerted effort to include multicultural voices within the news.[50]

One answer to the lack of diversity within news sources may be found with digital media and community journalism. Kurpius posits that community or civic journalism counteracts the mass media focus on white, male, elite sources. When evaluating community reporters' news coverage, Kurpius found nonminority journalists progressed in including more diverse audiences within their stories and were able to incorporate more minority sources. Civic journalism engages those within the community who are seeking change and want to speak out about community topics—allowing for a greater understanding of overall communal values and issues. The goal of civic journalism is for reporters to speak with everyday citizens instead of the overreliance on elite officials that dominates mainstream coverage.[51]

Instead of focusing on individuals or small communities like civic journalists, major news organizations search for sensationalized characters that will improve ratings.[52] Media prioritize stories revolving around drama, conflict, and controversy.[53] News directors determine what is newsworthy through a process called gatekeeping, a process of controlling what will air based on what they feel *their* viewers will watch. Widely viewed stories, regardless of accuracy or meaningfulness, translate into advertising dollars.[54] Therefore, concentration on profit makes some people more vulnerable, including viewers watching, sources interviewed, advertisers, and journalists who are at times controlled by their ownership groups.

News Routines and Minority Audiences

The norms and routines of mainstream journalism contribute to misrepresentation of minority audiences and, specifically, American Indians.[55] Mainstream news coverage often ignores social problems, covers through a conflict frame, and simplifies complex situations into stereotypes. In two trusted national papers, the *New York Times* and *Los Angeles Times* from 1999 to 2000, Seymour found that journalists placed terms that are normally acceptable, such as "American Indian," "tribe," and "reservation," out of context and thus used them in an offensive manner, for example, noting the Census Bureau records some "reservations as rancheras." Seymour writes, "Silly Indians. Why would they object to their national territory being likened to a cattle pen?," noting that the writer "fell into a self-made trap as it attempted to describe 4.1 million American Indians (as of the U.S. Census of 2000) as a single group."[56]

Seymour argues that this was careless journalism instead of outright racism—essentially lack of knowledge about the community since it is not necessarily considered an important beat.[57] The manner in which journalists reported on stories displayed little understanding or concern about Native identity and law, lumping all American Indians together. The news coverage the journalists produced perpetuated stereotypes and misrepresentation of the Native community to non-Native audiences.

Journalists, when faced with unknown territories, go into norms and routines mode to cover stories—including the use of historically negative stereotypes.[58] The deployment of routine allows journalists to know what stories, sources, and frames they should incorporate within news to fit the standards of media success.[59] Stereotypes reinforce images of a group and serve as mental shortcuts to easily understand a complicated matter—for example, the conflict frame typically positions minorities as dark villains that are threats to white ideologies.[60]

Stereotyping is a "conventional, formulaic, and oversimplified conception, opinion, or image," a way to bring a large collective audience into agreement.[61] New consumers have a structure system in their heads that serves as a schema.[62] Individuals are confused, often ignoring the narrative if it is constructed in a manner that does not fit the preconceived schema. Consequently, the same stereotypes and stories are accepted and told over and over again within our society.[63] It is cognitively efficient for non-Native news consumers to resort to stereotypical schemas when addressing American Indians.[64]

Because non-Natives have learned about American Indians through the media since the 1600s,[65] Natives were most commonly categorized as non-Christian barbarians and placed in the "them/other" category.[66] A noble savage was a Native person who agreed with the ideology that supported the beliefs of the settlers at that time.[67] Even today mainstream media continue to show American Indians as noble savages and/or barbarians and further implement these views by placing them within two media categories, "zoo stories" or "frozen in the past."[68] Zoo stories are those in which the media place a group on display. In the case of American Indians, these stories are often cultural events such as PowWows. The other category in which Natives are displayed is "frozen in the past"; this makes American Indians appear stuck in either poverty, alcoholism, and/or other problems detrimental to society.[69]

The overall medium of television focuses on the aforementioned visuals and stereotypical images for entertainment.[70] Viewers are often shown dramatic, seductive, and not always accurate images.[71] The good news is that some progress is evident in television and movies concerning imagery depicting American Indians. Hollywood, now, tries to embrace American Indian actors and directors and appears to be working toward an accurate portrayal of history.[72]

Although recent strides are encouraging, entertainment programming has been a stereotype breeding ground over the past one hundred years.[73] Highly educated and often young audiences turn to entertainment programming as information sources.[74] Television's goal is to entertain and amuse as much as it is to inform.[75] Television programs, with embedded symbols of value and morality, craft an exaggerated stereotypical view for those who watch it heavily.[76] For example, in the 1930s, the noble savage reared its stereotypical head in the radio show *The Lone Ranger*, which later moved to television. Tonto was the "faithful Indian companion" who dutifully supported the white status quo.[77]

American Indians are not the only minority group depicted through stereotypes. From the 1930s to 1950s, Hollywood cast African Americans in entertainment roles and inferior roles for "comedy."[78] Meanwhile, Latino stereotyping was centered on economic relations. In Latin American countries, sales of movies grew so large Hollywood created characters it hoped appealed to both the U.S. and foreign markets. The overseas sales shifted the "greaser" stereotype from the 1920s to the Latin Lover of the 1930s.[79]

Widely used and media-reinforced racial stereotypes such as the "noble savage" hinder a multicultural, democratic society by encouraging a limited viewpoint.[80]

Media determine a certain voice is more authentic, and subsequently more important, than others they deem inferior. Thus, the American Indian becomes marginalized to the views that society has already said are accepted, and the group becomes naturalized within society in stereotypical roles.[81]

Entman and Rojecki posit that the visual nature of race accounts for people's awareness;[82] in other words, most people don't centrally process race on a frequent basis, rather when it becomes portrayed visually or when issues connected with those races are narrated in implicit and explicit forms.[83] Typically, individuals view others who are racially different from them and try to gauge if they intend to inflict harm and then whether they have the ability to follow through with those intentions.[84] Historically, minorities are either framed negatively within television news or ignored altogether; thus, nonwhites are typically presented as a barrier to white safety.[85]

Cultural perceptions of what race means are socially constructed through the media and other influences such as family, community, education, and geographic location. How a person represents, interprets, and make sense of race helps build a personal ideology: an individual's reality-interpreting lens crafted by their values and beliefs. In the case of minorities, there is often a "white of the eye" ideology, in which minorities are viewed through a white lens. Hall identified two types of media articulations of race: overt and inferential racism.[86] Overt racism is direct, negative, obvious castigations of race; for instance, the use of common derogatory racial slurs would be overt. On the other hand, inferential racism, or subtle racial messages with hidden racial undercurrents and cues, can be more insidious. Because our society now desires more egalitarianism, overtly racist messages are normally rejected by the audiences because they undermine our culture's hope for equality. However, inferential racism often goes unnoticed and triggers previously dormant racial attitudes those in the audience didn't know they possessed.[87]

Historically, these overt and inferential messages have plagued mainstream media coverage of minorities, leading to many inaccuracies and destabilizing mainstream media's primary function of reporting truth.[88] For example, while covering crime, media often have an antiblack perspective. African Americans are typically shown as the group committing the crime and whites as victims, even though, statistically, these portrayals are not proportionately accurate—far fewer African Americans commit the crimes the news coverage suggests.[89] An explanation for this misrepresentation is twofold: the majority of media managers are white, and the managers are catering to a primarily white audience.[90]

Women face a similar scenario in the newsroom, as even modern-day newsrooms typically do not employ or promote women in newsrooms, much less multiracial women. Minority female journalists noted that they feel treated unfairly compared to their male counterparts who direct hostility toward them in the newsroom. Minority women journalists have said that they focus on their goals and not the discrimination and have expressed hopes that digital media may ameliorate some of these tensions.[91]

Digital media provide an opportunity for diversity, but depending on the content producer they may also reinforce stereotypical roles and images. In a study examining images on YouTube, Kopacz and Lawton coded for the role of American Indians speaking. While American Indians spoke within clips, most American Indians were not introduced to their audience and therefore their visibility was considered anonymous. Along with no acknowledgement, more than 84 percent of the videos did not mention the discrimination of the culture. The images shown of American Indians were predominantly male, and the authors said the mainstream needed to dump images of American Indians relying on the barbarian and the noble savage stereotypes that socially construct American Indians as savagely inferior and as excess baggage.[92]

In addition to digital media, advertising contributes to this racial degradation as well. American Indian stereotypes are often used as brands designed to sell products. Reducing a culture to a product encourages non-Natives to treat Native people as objects rather than fellow humans. By treating American Indians as items, society judges them as a possession that can be bought at will and discarded when no longer valuable.[93] For example, the Land O'Lakes logo is a stereotypical image of a woman kneeling to a lesser power position in society.[94] Images of American Indians in advertising also include the reader "playing Indian" or the image of the Indian to portray something "exotic."[95] Both of these images distance readers by having them "play" a culture or an unnatural role. Therefore, the concept of the American Indian becomes again an experience to sell.[96] From the PowWows to the sports mascot to the "cigar Indian," these accepted images become naturalized within white culture; if not, white culture would not permit the use of these images.[97]

American Indians are so forcefully exploited by advertising because the profit-driven industry is concerned with targeting the mass audience, not the 1 percent. However, this group is relatively young and growing. The Native population had a 17.2 percent purchasing power gain compared to other minorities such as African

Americans (10.2 percent) and whites (7 percent). American Indians are a relatively young group with a median age of 32 compared to whites at 39.2. Purchasing power for American Indians currently is 0.6 percent and equals $64.7 billion. Native purchasing power is expected to continuing growing.[98]

If advertisers and the media want to stay relevant, they will have to adjust to America's rapidly changing demographics.[99] The racial composition of the United States is changing so that the white majority is projected to become a minority by 2050.[100] Over the past ten years, people of color added twenty-seven million persons to the overall population.[101]

Mass media treat minority audiences as a "fringe audience"—an audience that does not directly affect their financial bottom line. The goal of the mainstream media is to produce content to attract a large similar group of people—hence the term "mass." In other words, mass media cover stories in a way that will attract the largest number of news consumers. The mainstream media reinforce the dominant European colonial ideology that has been around since the 1600s instead of challenging this view of American Indians and running the risk of alienating the mass audience.[102]

Increasing Native Journalists and Elevating Visibility

One proposed solution to counter stereotypical images of American Indians in mainstream and non-Native media is for mainstream media to reach out to Native news organizations and to increase the voices of those who are Native within mainstream news organizations. In the mainstream media in 2000, there were only 292 American Indian newspaper journalists of 56,200 total, because of the "complex cultural, social, educational and linguistic barriers erected and welded into place by our history."[103] Some scholars note that because of these barriers, Natives do not even consider journalism as a career.[104]

Another proposed solution is improved education, such as multiculturalism courses in college journalism schools that would require more American Indian inclusion in journalism. Some scholars have argued that those who are American Indian should focus on producing research rather than being a subject in a non-Native person's project. Native scholars who relay their experiences and their way of life allow for a more accurate depiction of American Indians to future scholars and to students.[105]

A clearer understanding of American Indian history is critical to education. To understand the importance of Native stories, non-Native readers must understand whose history is recorded within the United States.[106] When the "founding fathers" drafted the Constitution, groups like women and minorities were not part of "We the People." When the founding fathers wrote about "all men" this meant white men.[107]

Clearly, the founding fathers, in the Constitution, established an in-group of white men and, subsequently, an out-group comprised of the "others" or minorities.[108] For instance, the United States has failed at fully honoring any treaties made with Natives, and American Indians have been the only group that the United States government actively sought, and legislated, to exterminate. Nearly sixty thousand people died as a result of the American Indian Removal Act of the 1830s that resulted in the Trail of Tears.[109] During the nineteenth century, the United States designed schools to "kill the Indian, save the man."[110] The last of these residential schools operated as late as 1989. Students were placed in schools often run by churches to "civilize" them and to rid them of their Native culture. These children were starved, sexually assaulted, forced to work, and tortured. Survivors often relied on alcohol and other drugs to cope, and some committed suicide. The trauma from these schools passed down from one generation to the next, and some believe resulted in spousal and child abuse.[111] This history, packaged quickly here in a few sentences for the sake of clarity, is essential for non-Native media professionals to understand to improve representations of American Indians.

Historians have written about what they feel is the unfair treatment of American Indians, but they have not set norms and routines for addressing this community.[112] Institutional review boards at some universities consider American Indians a sensitive research group, in the same category as young children and pregnant women, because this group has been treated so poorly.[113] The sensitivity of this group also extends to how Natives are exploited in the press and should address how the media should or should not cover sacred events such as ceremonies and typically open events such as PowWows.[114]

The history of American Indians has been written mostly by white males who haven't asked those who are Native what they think.[115] Since colonial times, Native history has been written by non-Natives—recording their interpretation of American Indian history for American Indians.[116] This has affected how people view American Indians and even how Native people view themselves and their surroundings.[117]

Excluding Native people in the recording of Native history may raise a moral and ethical dilemma.[118] Authentic perspectives allow more accurate research and depictions of minority communities, counteracting the outsiders' perspective.[119] Some historians have treated Native people as the "other," different from writers and readers. These same historians did not interview Native people for historical records.[120]

The stereotypical and invisible display of American Indians goes back to the first paper published in the United States, *Publick Occurrences* (1690). The first issue reported on the "savages" that threatened their existence.[121] Reporting about "savages" represented a colonial view that assumed the reader was part of the dominant societal group.[122]

The painful past, often ignored by whites, sets the stage for continuing impact on communities. For example, one of the worst crimes against Natives occurred during the 1862 U.S.–Dakota War. Thirty-eight men were hanged, and thousands of people were made captive on the Dakota reservation in Minnesota. The United States then abolished the Dakota reservation area and forced the tribe into Nebraska and South Dakota.[123]

To this day, while the Dakota community's health and living conditions have improved, the community is still recovering.[124] The latest U.S. census numbers on the Pine Ridge reservation in South Dakota are more than a decade old, which is telling in itself. Demographic data-collection on American Indian communities is not always reliable in part because of inconsistent definitions.[125] Pine Ridge is considered the nation's poorest reservation, located in three of the poorest counties in the United States. Individuals living on this reservation are eight times more likely to get diabetes and/or tuberculosis, five times more likely to get cervical cancer, and twice as likely to get heart disease. One in four newborns have fetal alcohol syndrome, and the infant mortality rate is three times the rate of the rest of the nation. The suicide rate is twice the national rate, four times higher for teens. Pine Ridge has the lowest life expectancy rate in the United States with Haiti being the only place in the Western Hemisphere with lower life expectancy.[126]

In response to such grim statistics, organizations such as the Native American Journalists Association (NAJA) have been training Native journalists in advancing coverage through digital media. The University of Oklahoma, along with the NAJA, has held annual new media conferences for Native journalists. In 2012, the focus of the one-day conference was on hearing from those within Native media who provide news by social media such as Tom Arviso, executive editor and publisher of the

Navajo Times, and Bryan Pollard, executive editor of the *Cherokee Phoenix*. In the second year of the conference, twenty-two participants learned a more hands-on approach to digital media such as how to use programs such as PhotoShop and InDesign as well as social media.[127]

Another proposed solution to rectify false images of American Indians is to incorporate Native media and Native voices. The history of the United States, and the relative exclusion of the American Indian side of that narrative, has been unsettling for the American Indian community—even more reason why many call for Natives to write about Native topics whether in journalism or in scholarly work. The inclusion of these Native voices, in both journalism and education, would allow for breadth and depth concerning the stories told about this community: "how the Indian narrative is told, how it is nourished, who tells it, who nourishes it, and the consequences of its telling are among the most fascinating—and, at the same time, chilling—stories of our time."[128]

In spite of their extensive heritage, Native voices are missing from history and from present research.[129] Non-Native authors are often cited and noted as the "experts" on Indian issues even though actual Natives are available. For this to change, tribal and family historians as well as other Natives should be asked about how they feel about what has been written and still needs to be discussed.[130]

Natives writing about Native issues provide an intellectual voice beyond stereotypes.[131] Even though American Indians proportionately served in the military at higher rates than any other minority group, when assessing images from World War II, the savage stereotype still remained. The one exception to this rule was the Navajo code talkers who were the antithesis to the savage stereotype.[132] Clearly, the barriers described here, a lack of desire for diversity in media, a lack of educational understanding of American Indian history, and a lack of Native voice inclusion, influence what decisions American Indians make about journalism as a whole.[133]

The field of journalism has made some attempts to incorporate American Indian attitudes toward the press. To provide American Indians with journalism opportunities, universities in Montana, North Dakota, South Dakota, and Wisconsin hold summer programs for Native high school students interested in journalism.[134] The Freedom Forum, a nonpartisan foundation that supports free press, speech, and spirit, hosts the annual American Indian Journalism Institute, in hopes of providing tools for young people to learn more about the discipline.[135] The University of Minnesota held a ten-week training and newspaper internship for those with a four-year degree in journalism; the students took classes for three days a week and then worked in area newspapers as reporters for two days. The Native American Newspaper Career Conference held in South Dakota had more than seventy high school students and created a mentoring programming with South Dakota newspapers and students. Many of these students will be the first generation in their family to go to college.[136]

CHAPTER 2

The Data

This research seeks to understand how Native news organizations that use digital media may be changing more traditional storytelling methods. Victoria conducted in-depth interviews with Native journalists and observed Native newsrooms. To identify which news organizations to observe and which Native journalists to interview, Victoria relied on professional organizations such as the Native American Journalists Association (NAJA) and snowball sampling. Victoria conducted interviews of Native journalists on the phone, in person, over e-mail, and through messages on social media.

In-Depth Interviews

In-depth interviews are appropriate as digital media are still evolving and therefore research in this area is exploratory. Digital media research, coupled with a focus on American Indian media, adds to this exploratory study because little research has been conducted on American Indian media. Thorough interviews enabled us to understand where to begin on a topic not yet fully studied, gather comprehensive background information, and develop a variety of inclusive topics relating to Native digital media.

The strength of qualitative interviews lies in the researcher's ability to immerse him/herself into a research setting and to provide detailed descriptions large news companies won't provide. The researcher conducting interviews builds a detailed description and treats each one as a "conversation with a purpose."[1] For this study, Victoria created a guideline she used while conducting interviews.[2]

In-depth interviews typically contain smaller sample sizes but provide great detail about the interviewees' opinions such as "values, motivations, recollections, experiences, and feelings."[3] The interviews are typically long, unlike survey research questions that may take only minutes to answer. In contrast to survey research, in-depth interviews may take hours for the researcher to gain a full understanding of the answers given.[4]

Another divergence from survey research is in-depth interviews do not generalize the overall population. The sample is typically nonrandom, and the data are used not to make statements about the entire population, but instead to generate insights on an unexplored topic.[5] This study hopes to provide as much detail, depth, and understanding as possible on American Indian digital media.

This research is exploratory and concerned with what the interviews mean culturally, not necessarily looking for overtly categorized quantitative descriptions. Therefore, qualitative thematic categories are a more conducive instrument for exploring Native storytelling within the context of digital media.

Snowball Sample

Victoria relied on snowball sampling in which the "researcher randomly contacts a few qualified respondents and then asks these people for names of friends, relatives, or acquaintances,"[6] within the American Indian community. Contacting authoritative figures for guidance greatly helped me effectively speak with a variety of people within the American Indian community.

The large number of subjects who contacted Victoria and expressed an eagerness to participate in the research was somewhat surprising. They indicated they wanted to participate with an American Indian student conducting American Indian research. Journalists and families from across the country contacted Victoria through e-mail, Facebook, Twitter, and Google+. American Indian news and professional organizations were especially supportive in recruitment. Native publications posted interview requests online, and the reviewer contacted other Native journalists with whom Victoria's current university had relationships. This helped her connect with several individuals through Native pages on Facebook.

Such networking proved incredibly helpful to this study. As Victoria spoke to Native journalists, they referred her to other American Indians who have made strides in the communication discipline. The snowball sample led Victoria to contact NAJA, of which she is a member. Victoria attended the Unity/NAJA conference in August 2012, following the summer where after she conducted most of my interviews. This Las Vegas conference enabled her to interview additional journalists about the future of Native media. The large number of American Indian and other minority journalists gathered in the same conference hall allowed Victoria to be inclusive in who was interviewed.

Multiple minority organizations, Native and others, had enthusiasm about this study and assisted with interview recruitment. Minority-focused research organizations such as Howard University and the Minority and Communication division of the Association for Education in Journalism and Mass Communication (AEJMC) placed this study's information on their organizations' e-mail circulation. Specific individuals from Howard and AEJMC also e-mailed Victoria to offer support and/or ideas about the research.

Victoria contacted multiple mainstream news organizations to seek assistance in finding research interviewees. She e-mailed the Poynter Institute, Knight Foundation, Scripps Research Institute, McCormick Foundation, and Pew Research Center for guidance in recruitment. These organizations were extremely helpful, but the main response and assistance from this research was within Native and minority organizations.

Research Process

Victoria's goal was to interview tribally independent Native news organizations and to speak with journalists from newspaper, radio, and television. She was able to visit and/or interview forty-one Native journalists from each of these mediums, and their interviews ranged from thirty minutes to three and a half hours.

In addition to interviewing of Native journalists on the phone, in person, over e-mail, and through messages on social media, Victoria spent a week in New

Mexico/Arizona where two of the largest Native news organizations are located. The Manship School of Mass Communication as well as Larry and Susan Patrick of Patrick Communications helped fund the research travel.

Face-to-face interactions were undoubtedly important to this research, but Facebook was also a crucial research method, which is telling of this study. If Victoria had a hard time getting in contact with a Native journalist by phone or e-mail, replies were nearly instant on Facebook and she received many instant Facebook replies when conducting follow-up questions for this study.

Thematic Analysis

To provide a transparent audit of the research process, Victoria first transcribed each interview. Second, she printed all of the interviews after transcription. Third, she placed the printed copy of the interviews into themes. Fourth, Victoria electronically rechecked the themes by searching for key terms within the Word file and by placing each of the hard copy themes in an overall organized folder with sections for each theme. Because the research is not quantitative she analyzed the transcripts multiple times for the themes to ensure accuracy.

Victoria tried multiple qualitative computer programs to evaluate the transcribed interviews; however, she found the most fruitful analysis process was listening to the interviews and typing each one herself. The interviews for this study resulted in 162 pages of transcription. The unit of analysis for this study was each interview. The frequencies for each theme are the following: twelve under history/context, ten under storytelling, ten under digital media, and nine under youth/future. The operationalized definition for each category along with an example from the data is included below. This is a qualitative project; however, we chose to include this more quantitative-like description for project transparency. During the several reviews of this project several mix-method researchers recommended this sort of transparency.

History/Context

History/context includes the background of American Indians and American Indian media that also details the importance of tribes, community, and culture.

One of the most basic things that I think a lot of mainstream journalists miss is that each tribe is unique. They have their own history. Their own traditions. They have their own ways, and their own cultural identity is succinct from all the other tribes. There may be similarities here and there.[7]

If something positive, you are going to have something negative so there is a lot of history here in journalism.[8]

Storytelling

Storytelling emphasized the importance of the role of language, storytelling, and authentic Native voices (Native people speaking about Native issues).

Storytelling is always changing by technology. Just the idea of the written word—as opposed to writing it down—has changed the nature of storytelling. The Internet is just another example of that.[9]

Storytelling is very important still to Native communities and the fact that Native stories aren't told by the mainstream media. You know, if we don't tell them who will? I think that it is really important to people that they are accurate and authentic Native stories about our communities whether they are urban or rural, as opposed to the kind of iconography that has developed around Indians.[10]

Digital Media

The digital media category discussed the impact of technology and digital platforms such as websites, podcasts, mobile applications (including live streaming), Facebook, and Twitter. This category also noted how this platform may allow for American Indian voices to surface within non-Native media and, therefore, combat Native stereotypes.

I think it is getting a little bit faster paced. With technology, everyone can go online and get whatever they want, but for the *Navajo Times* in particular, I think it is steady.[11]

For one thing new media, new technology allows us to tell our story quicker.[12]

With the development of new technology, a lot of the stations are podcasting so we just upload all our programs on there so they can download them.[13]

Youth/Future

Lastly, the category of youth/future emerged from the discussion of digital media and digital media/stereotypes. Native journalists noted the importance of Native youth voices in tribal and non-Native newsrooms as media move to digital platforms.

> More youth must be encouraged to learn what I know, although I have personally trained twenty editors and they are now working elsewhere.[14]
>
> We started another young lady this morning. She is going to the University of New Mexico. She has good writing talent. So I said let's take a chance on her. Let's see what we can do. We have three interns here. College interns working now. Actually four. We hired another lady working in our graphics departments. So we have four students here, all Navajos, that we think really have talent and basic ability to write and do their graphics so we are encouraging them to stay in the field so that's a big part of what we do.[15]

Interviews

Victoria created a guide for interviews for this study (see appendix), but as qualitative scholars suggest, she approached interviews with a delicate balance of asking questions and then asking follow-up questions arising from the interview.[16] These questions probed journalists about their thoughts on how Native media may be changing with digital platforms and how this may or may not be advancing understanding of the Native community.

Participant Observation

Along with interviews, Victoria attempted to be a "fly on the wall" as she visited Native news organizations. At the *Navajo Times*, she had her own desk located among the reporters, and was able to witness how journalists went about covering stories and hear how stories changed before publication. While Victoria spent most of her time at the *Navajo Times*, she also attempted to immerse herself in the surroundings of the Koahnic Broadcast Corporation's Albuquerque offices.

Victoria attempted to be a "participant-as-observer," where she was aware of the actions that took place within a newsroom but did not become fully involved in the routine.[17] Lindlof and Taylor posit a major part of participant observation is to understand the language used within the scene. Since Victoria has a Native background and worked in newspaper, radio, and television, we feel her experience and cultural awareness allowed her to grasp some of the routines observed within American Indian media. Victoria took diligent notes during the interview and observation stages of the research, and as Lindlof and Taylor recommend, she kept multiple journals filled with notes as she conducted this research.[18]

Native Journalists Interviewed

Lindlof and Taylor explain it is essential for a researcher to receive at least a tentative agreement from a gatekeeper in a newsroom.[19] Trusting their expertise, Victoria contacted news managers at the *Navajo Times*, Koahnic Broadcast Corporation (KBC), and Indian Country TV for permission to visit and interview employees and interviewed Native journalists within these organizations who had influence on the overall Native news product. We believe it is crucial to interview not just journalists with bylines or experience in front of the camera, but also as many news workers as possible to understand why news is produced in its final form. Interviewees included news managers, reporters, producers, anchors, photographers, graphic design artists, and news production.

Researcher Obligation

We understand researcher obligation concerning project transparency.[20] This obligation is especially important within the American Indian community since it has often been misrepresented. Therefore, Victoria received Louisiana State University institutional review board approval, where she was a PhD candidate at the time, before conducting interviews for this project and e-mailed those she interviewed with study information and a confidentiality statement.

Main Native Organizations Visited

Navajo Times

The *Navajo Times* is a tribally independent for-profit newspaper located in Window Rock, Arizona. The Navajo Tribal Council along with the Bureau of Indian Affairs and Department of Education started this paper as a newsletter in 1959. A year later, the council published it in a newspaper form.[21] While the paper started as a weekly, it did publish daily for three years but, because it couldn't financially survive in this form, returned to a weekly publication. The *Navajo Times* has the largest circulation of *all* American Indian papers at close to twenty-five thousand subscribers and estimates the electronic edition and website attract around 150,000 readers a week.[22]

The paper's mission is first to inform the Navajo people, the Native community, and then the rest of the world. The Navajo Nation does not control the news content or editorials in the paper. However, the newspaper operates and adheres to the laws of the Navajo Nation, including equal rights for men and women and "freedom of religion, speech, press, and the right of assembly."[23]

The *Navajo Times* executive officer and publisher, Tom Arviso, recommended Victoria visit the paper in Window Rock, Arizona, during the "Healing the Earth Gathering" held the third week of June 2012. The event was scheduled to be held in Flagstaff, Arizona, near the San Francisco Peaks at one of the Navajo Nation's four sacred mountains.[24] However, because of what are believed to be issues with the water settlement in the area, the annual festival did not take place. The cancellation of this festival did not occur until after Victoria was already on the reservation. Interestingly, the cancelling of the event may be just as important a part of this area's story as if it had taken place and will be discussed later in this study.

The *Navajo Times* staff consists of thirty people including eight reporters, two of whom are non-Native and freelance for the paper. Prominent Native journalists interviewed include Tom Arviso, Navajo, CEO and Publisher, and Marley Shebala, Navajo, an award-winning senior reporter. Arviso, a graduate of Arizona State University, is known for separating the *Navajo Times* from tribal control and Shebala for her investigations of tribal presidents' misuse of funds.[25]

Koahnic Broadcast Corporation

KBC is a nonprofit Alaska broadcast company located in Anchorage. "Koahnic" is an Athabascan word in the Ahtna dialect meaning "live air."[26] The corporation's mission is to become the leader in bringing Native voices to Alaska and the nation. KBC has nearly twenty paid employees and, at its Anchorage-based radio station KNBA, twenty-one volunteer radio hosts.

The primary KBC journalists interviewed were Antonia Gonzales, Navajo, anchor/producer of *National Native News*; Will Kie, Pueblo, associate producer of *Native America Calling*; and Joaqlin Estus, Tlingit, news director at KNBA.

Burt Poley is a Hopi/Laguna radio journalist and former network manager at KBC's Native Voice One (NV1) distribution network located in Albuquerque, New Mexico. Poley contacted Victoria through the snowball sample, and she received his permission to visit NV1's Albuquerque facilities.[27] Victoria visited NV1's downtown Albuquerque facilities when she visited the *Navajo Times*, since these two media organizations are geographically within three hours of each other by car.

There are six permanent KBC employees in its Albuquerque branch. Three employees are American Indian, with multiple tribal bloodlines including Pueblo and Navajo. The other three employees are non-Native.[28] KBC's satellite office operates two national news services and a national program distribution service serving Native radio stations across the country. KBC produces *National Native News*, a daily five-minute news program, *Native America Calling*, a one-hour daily call-in show, and *Earthsongs*, a weekly one-hour music/talk show. The corporation also airs occasional one-hour radio documentaries. NV1 distributes these programs to more than two hundred radio stations across the country.[29]

NV1 enables Native people, especially those who do not have access to the many reservation- and village-based Native owned-and-operated stations, to stay connected to Native news. Many Native stations and independent radio producers contribute Native-oriented programs to NV1 for inclusion in the NV1 program service.[30]

Indian Country Communications

The last organization Victoria had planned to visit was Indian Country Communications in Hayward, Wisconsin; however, multiple arson fires the week before her visit cancelled our plans.[31] Executive director Paul DeMain was hunting in the woods at the time of the fire and was not harmed. The fires burned down a recreational vehicle that served as his home, a covered wigwam structure sitting outside of the news organization. The building that housed Indian Country Communications suffered fire damage as did a ceremonial lodge and trading post.[32] The fires destroyed three buildings and severely damaged another. The night before this set of fires another fire burned down the Golden Eagle sweat lodge.[33] In replacement of this trip, Victoria interviewed DeMain on the phone and corresponded with him and his staff through e-mail and social media, and he recommended Victoria visit during the "Honor of the Earth PowWow," as there is a huge gathering during this time.[34]

Paul DeMain, Oneida/Ojibwe, is a well-known Native journalist and past president of the NAJA; he is well respected by the NAJA who recommended Victoria visit his news organization. DeMain was also a past president of the NAJA and is a member of several Native ceremonial societies. Another journalist Victoria interviewed was Josh Pearson, Ojibwe, Lac Courte Oreilles, a web producer/editor and student at the University of Wisconsin–Green Bay.

Indian Country Communications publishes the newspaper *News from Indian Country* (*NFIC*) and Indian Country TV. *NFIC* is a national Native newspaper and has fourteen issues a year, each available electronically. Its sister media component, Indian Country TV, includes an online news site, a daily video news segment distributed through social media and e-mail, and a mobile application.

Additional Journalists

In addition to interviews conducted with the *Navajo Times*, KBC, and Indian Country Communications, below is a list of other key journalists interviewed.

- Mark Trahant, Shoshone-Bannock, writer, author, speaker, and Twitter poet. Past instructor at University of Idaho and University of Colorado at Boulder, former editor for the *Seattle Post-Intelligence*, former columnist at the *Seattle Times*, publisher of the *Moscow-Pullman Daily News* in Moscow, Idaho; executive news editor of the *Salt Lake Tribune*; a reporter at the *Arizona Republic* in Phoenix; and has worked at several tribal newspapers. Chairman and chief executive officer at the Robert C. Maynard Institute for Journalism Education and past president of the NAJA
- Patty Talahongva, Hopi, multimedia producer including documentaries for HBO and the National Museum of the American Indian, thirty years as a journalist, including working as a reporter for KOOL-TV/Phoenix (local CBS station) and past president of the NAJA
- Bryan Pollard, Cherokee, executive editor, *Cherokee Phoenix*; cofounder/ former managing editor of *Street Roots*, a monthly tabloid focused on

poverty issues in Portland, Oregon; photo editor at the Oklahoma Institute
for Diversity in Journalism. Board member at the North American Street
Newspaper Association, and Louisiana State University graduate

- Shirley Kay Sneve, Sicangu Lakota, executive director, Vision Maker Media
(formerly Native American Public Telecommunications, Inc.), whose
mission is to share Native stories with the world that represent the cultures,
experiences, and values of American Indians and Alaska Natives. Board
member for the Association of American Cultures and the Arts Extension
Institute, and former producer for South Dakota Public Broadcasting
- Peggy Berryhill, Muskogee (Creek), president/general manager, KGUA/Pomo,
California; award-winning producer and founder/president of the Native
Media Resource Center, a nonprofit organization that produces Indigenous
educational content to promote cross-cultural harmony
- Rhonda LeValdo, Acoma Pueblo, president, NAJA; faculty in Media
Communications at Haskell Indian Nations University; producer for Native
Spirit Radio at 90.1 FM-KKFI/Kansas City, MO; and reporter for *National
Native News* and Native News Network
- Chase Iron Eyes, Lakota, creator, LastRealindians.com, and attorney, graduate
of law at University of Denver

CHAPTER 3

Helping Native Voices Breathe

To discover how digital media influence Native media, this analysis first seeks to understand the connection between the ritual of Native storytelling and Native news coverage. Second, this research explores whether digital media are advancing the ritual of storytelling. Third, the research addresses whether Native journalists feel digital media are increasing American Indian voices as part of the storytelling ritual. Finally, this study discusses how digital media may help provide a more multifaceted view of the Native community: by providing more voices from this community and by digital media possibly increasing the number of Native journalists working in the business. This analysis begins with organizational details of the Native media included in this study to convey the diversity of Native news outlets and the similarities and differences with mainstream media.

Inside the Native Press

We wanted to first understand *who* comprises Native media to set the scene for the rest of the analysis. Below are details on ownership and staff size for each Native organization as they may affect the news produced and therefore the news consumers receive. An interesting note is that most Native news organizations are nonprofit, and these organizations define profit as providing authentic Native news to its community.

To answer the book's research questions, a story must first be told about the journey of visiting, observing, and interviewing Native journalists across the country. This story began with the primary Native media outlet interviewed for this study, the *Navajo Times*. The newsroom is approximately three hours from Albuquerque, New Mexico, in Window Rock, Arizona. On this drive, the interstate was surrounded by colors of the sun—orange and red mountains in the distance. In juxtaposition to this natural scene, billboards lined the sky, one with an advertisement that promotes the *Navajo Times* website.

A straight interstate, I-40 west, leads to the newspaper. Twelve miles from the newspaper drivers find a fork, forcing a decision to go left or right. Steering left connects to Indian Route 12 where the Navajo reservation is located. The newspaper's office is on the right side of the road at the entrance of the reservation. Across the street from the paper is a flea market where residents sell clothes, books, bikes, and treats such as snow cones and golden pine nuts or piñons. Piñons are popular on the reservation. Historically they were traded as currency at posts. The significance of the flea market is later understood on this trip, as the market brought up childhood memories for those working at the paper. Alastair Bitsoi, a *Navajo Times* reporter, shared a story of gathering pine nuts at his grandmother's home. Another *Navajo Times* reporter, Noel Lyn Smith, had a good-humored childhood rule—she only bought snow cones at the flea market and candy apples at the trading post.

Back across the street from the flea market, the *Navajo Times* is located in a small strip of businesses. The front of the newspaper building holds a dusty *Navajo Times* sign. As Victoria pulled up to the newspaper in my silver rental car, she noticed a horse had been in that same parking spot before her. The newspaper recommended a rental car could handle the rougher reservation roads; the choice between a generic-looking silver car or a small sporty red car was an easy one.

Outside on the right of the paper is the reservation's Indian Health Clinic. Behind the newspaper, the sky is lined with red sandstone rock. Window Rock gets its name from a circle-like window in the middle of a large piece of red rock behind the tribal offices on the Navajo reservation. As you hear the assembly line of the press running at the *Navajo Times*, the back door of the paper opens up to reveal the red-clay-colored rocks that line the sky, a very symbolic scene reminiscent of the Navajo journalists' discussion of the sacred mountains in Flagstaff. Perhaps this is a natural reminder of the community's sacredness, as the paper's printing press records the Navajo people's history.

> We are here to provide a service to our people. To be a communication source. To let them know what is going on with their government, their schools, their communities, what's going on in the outside world. That's our first and foremost reason for why we exist.[1]

To give a sense of the atmosphere at the *Navajo Times*, when you enter the newspaper you hear the sounds of the Navajo language on the radio. The receptionist is listening and sometimes singing along in Navajo. At the time of Victoria's visit, the *Navajo Times* had a partnership with the radio station through which it recorded news headlines in the morning that were aired several times throughout the day.

The newspaper serves as more than a source of information; it also is a communal gathering place. Every morning, Navajo residents come in to sell items to newspaper employees. Little girls sell apples dipped in red cinnamon candy for a dollar. Vendors also sell in the newsroom a Navajo breakfast staple, blue mush that is even sold at the reservation's gas stations. Reporters recommended Victoria add some sugar to the mush that vendors keep hot in coolers and then sell in a Styrofoam cup with a spoon. Some journalists preferred the blue grit-like staple cooked with ash, as it reminded them of their grandmother's food. Other mornings for breakfast you could buy homemade tamales wrapped in corn silks. The tamales would make you never eat this food again in a restaurant or from a can because they taste much better. There were also jewelry vendors. One artist sold her a bird necklace and gave Victoria the earrings that matched because she was visiting the Navajo Nation. "They feel comfortable selling to us, but they also visit."[2]

Sometimes elderly people also would come in to the newspaper because they were lonely, while other residents would visit to size up the paper's operation to evaluate if they wanted to share a potential news story. Along with having an open door to the community, the paper also supports the reservation by giving free subscriptions to military personnel away from home. "It is the least we can do to send them the *Navajo Times* so they have that connection at home."[3] The military has a strong connection to the Navajo tribe dating back, at least, to the Navajo code talkers who were integral during World War II. The paper also sends free subscriptions to prisoners who can't afford it as "they are paying the price for whatever they have done wrong, but they still have that connection to us."[4]

Budget cuts have left most of the schools on the reservation without a newspaper. At one time, the *Navajo Times* printed all of the school newspapers. Many at this press were saddened that media weren't as prevalent on the reservation as they used to be. The *Navajo Times* attempts to bridge the gap that the budget cuts have left by working with schools to give them a discount on the paper so that youth can learn about local current events.

Inside the *Navajo Times*, the newsroom looked quite new. The current office is the paper's second location. The former location was across the street near the flea market. Much like a mainstream newsroom, the newspaper's space is compartmentalized. To the right is the publisher, human resources, and circulation. To the left, the reporters and editors have their desks. Shortly down a hall, the editor sits essentially in the center of the overall building. In the back of the newspaper are the graphic, photography, sales, and printing departments.

The *Navajo Times* is the largest Native American paper and the only Native newspaper that has a printing press in-house. The paper has subscribers around the world with a paid circulation of twenty-five thousand readers. The paper said its paid circulation really isn't that much considering there are more than three hundred thousand Navajos; however, it estimates that with the *Navajo Times*'s electronic edition that subscribers receive via e-mail and its website it has is close to 150,000 readers a week.

The paper's coverage area is large, about the size of the state of West Virginia. The area includes the widespread Navajo Nation and the four corners that make up the border towns touching the reservation. There is symbolism in the paper covering these four corners. The Navajos have ceremonies for each of the four seasons.[5] The paper had the first four-color system in the area, and the first item printed was a specialized cartoon by Charles Schulz on Christmas Day 1982.[6] The overall Native flag includes four colors: red, white, yellow, and black. Each color represents the compass directions: north, south, east, and west.[7]

The paper has ten delivery drivers who leave early Thursday morning and drop off papers throughout Arizona, Utah, New Mexico, and Colorado. Once the paper is printed, carriers line the paper's hallway between the circulation department and the printing press. Navajo music played on a boom box and the smell of ink filled the rooms as women and male teens wore rubber gloves to avoid ink-stained hands as they placed advertising inserts into each of the papers.

Paul Natonabah, head photographer, has been at the *Navajo Times* longer than its current printing press and is nicknamed "Mr. *Navajo Times*" by the staff. Natonabah went to school in Chicago and studied commercial art for two years. He then returned to the reservation to work at the office of equal economic opportunity (EEO), and his work led him to the *Navajo Times*. Natonabah designed posters and pamphlets at the EEO. He helped a man named Chuck McCrory, who produced the newsletters, with photos, taking pictures on a Polaroid camera. After the 1970 national election, McCrory hired Natonabah at the *Navajo Times*.

Natonabah's newspaper office reflects the history of the paper. Behind a closed door to the right of Natonabah's desk is the old darkroom he designed himself. The darkroom's door has long been shut, and Natonabah crops and color-corrects photos digitally on his computer.

Time not only changed how Natonabah edited pictures, but also the enterprise of the paper. "The good thing that happened was the paper finally separated from the tribe."[8] Natonabah said the tribal government separation increased the paper's circulation and therefore revenue. He explained that before the separation, the paper had to submit its budget to the tribal council. "All the money we made went back to the tribe. If we needed equipment or something we had to go through all this red tape."[9]

The *Navajo Times* started as a newsletter in the late 1950s and became a paper at the start of the 1960s. The Bureau of Indian Affairs, the Department of Education, and tribal officials thought it should start a newspaper to inform the community about tribal events.[10] In 1960, the newsletter became a newspaper and was copyrighted as the *Navajo Times*. The first issue came out in August 1960 and cost ten cents. Today, it costs ten times this much—a dollar. Starting in 1984, the paper was a Monday-through-Friday publication and changed its name to the *Navajo Times Today*. Three years later it changed its name back to the *Navajo Times* when it went back to being a weekly.[11]

The *Navajo Times* survived what several call the 1989 civil war in Window Rock. Allegations against then chairman Peter MacDonald caused a deadly riot in the streets of Window Rock.[12]

Our newspaper was critical of Peter MacDonald, how he campaigned and some of his business dealings he had had in prior administrations, so he wasn't too crazy about us. One of the first things he did when he got in office was he had our finances looked at, investigated, and basically used that to shut us down.[13]

The paper received threats, including burning down its building. "When the riot happened that was one of the saddest days in the history of our Navajo people—we are actually killing each other over politics."[14] The paper reopened after three to four months. When the paper started printing again, MacDonald hired a new staff. "It started as a publication where he could do no wrong. A newsletter just for him."[15]

After the Navajo tribal council placed MacDonald on administrative leave, the paper was restaffed again, adding Tom Arviso as executive officer and publisher. "I was in the right place at the right time. I then changed the *Navajo Times* back to being a real newspaper, covering all sides of stories and promoting free press."[16] MacDonald was later sent to federal prison on crimes connected to fraud and bribery.[17]

With the history of the paper and the battles it fought to publish, as a researcher Victoria attempted to establish trust before the interviews. The first thing the publisher and Victoria did was sit down with two additional news gatekeepers: the newspaper editor and the human resources manager. The three men and Victoria sat around a table in the publisher's office where the resume that she sent to the paper months earlier lay on the table.

A connection Victoria instantly felt at the *Navajo Times* reflected a different in-group community: the newsroom. The men at the table were the same age or a little older than an adult's father figure, and Victoria sat as an outsider. Even if one is Native and/or grew up aware of Native culture, that individual is still considered an outsider because he or she was not raised in the visited community. Victoria had worked as a journalist for thirteen years, including newspaper. She also had worked in television consultation for six years where she visited stations across the country and worked with international networks.

Sitting in this meeting at the *Navajo Times* reminded her of the first time she would go into a television station for consultation. In the industry, consulting is synonymous with people getting fired. Often the anchors, who tended to be seasoned and had more years of experience, would cautiously look at Victoria and wonder what she was going to say. Even then, the mutual goal was for information to be clearly communicated to an audience as digital platforms changed, and therefore the staff soon realized Victoria was not a threat.

In Window Rock, the three news gatekeepers and Victoria discussed the goals of my research. A goal of the research process was to provide transparency within a community historically ignored and/or mistreated. Victoria spoke with the publisher several times before her visit. She offered to share anything she wrote with those in the newsroom to make sure she recorded the information in the correct context.

Today, the *Navajo Times* has a staff of more than thirty. Before Victoria conducted her first interview, the publisher walked her through the newsroom and personally introduced her to every person in the building. He explained who she was and the type of research she was hoping to conduct. He noted Victoria wasn't being offensive if she was staring or watching the newspaper workers as they went through their daily routines.

By the end of the week, Victoria was able to witness the inner workings of the paper and was accepted as an outside visitor. Following my week at the paper, the journalists whom she had observed arranged a lunch for her at the flea market. They all walked across the street and ate fry bread, mutton, squash, and for dessert, a snow cone. What they didn't eat was set outside to feed the reservation dogs roaming freely around town. The lunch was an adventure in itself as one of the long-time senior reporters bought a purple bike at the flea market and whizzed past them as they walked back to the paper following the lunch. Victoria's stay on the reservation, appropriately, went full circle: from an outsider just seeing the flea market across the street from the paper to having a good-bye dinner there with the *Navajo Times* staff.

Unlike mainstream media, Native media focus on the *entire* community. The word "community" is not isolated to one person or one neighborhood. A larger thought is in place, and the overall Native community belief is that behavior happening at the microlevel affects the macro universe. Culturally, it is understood one incident is not isolated but connected to all living things. One example, discussed later in this analysis, is a story about the reservation water shortage and how horses are not receiving adequate water. The suffering of the horses, according to those Victoria observed and interviewed, will come back full circle and hurt the entire community and culture that allowed it to occur.[18]

The Navajo people historically were sheep herders. The Churro-sheep are included on the Navajo flag and seal. On the reservation, this image appears on many tribal government vehicles. The importance of this animal is deeply rooted and conveys the connection with nature.

> People who really have a concern and take care of their animals of course they understand the relationship with the animals, and animals understand their relationship with the human people. It comes from both sides. And all livestock, all

animals are like that. They can tell when someone cares about them. When there
is an actual relationship going on.[19]

The importance of animals was visually clear around the reservation. For example,
the Navajo reservation has a zoo and even a veterinarian and livestock program.

The connection with community, nature, and life also lies in religion. The
religious experience, or church, for many Native people is stepping outside and
connecting with nature. Nature is what some outsiders may consider American
Indian people's place of worship with all its balanced elements. It is believed that
not doing what is best for all things means harm not only to the community but
to the Creator.

Everything is connected—Father Sky, Mother Earth, the sun, and all the
elements: earth, air, fire, and water.[20] All these natural elements make up the world
in which Native people live every day. These elements are part of who a person is
and even what he/she writes about as a journalist. Even saying "God Bless America,"
Navajo Times senior reporter Marley Shebala said, is interesting to think about
because the Navajo people believe in blessing the *entire* universe, supporting the
full circle collective thinking.

Within the Native media, the overall good is so understood that there is
concern for those who are being reported on and how they connect to the state of
the community. In mainstream media, the focus is on breaking stories and putting
an individual face to a story. Story coverage, however, is different in Native media.
The Navajo community understands if an everyday person commits a crime such
as sexual assault, a safe place to heal this event is in a tribal ceremony, not in the
media. In terms of privacy, families are respected if a tragic event occurs, and it is
culturally understood there will be an "airing out of events" in a ceremonial way.[21]
This cultural community style of reporting will be further discussed later in this
analysis.

Native News

In mainstream society everything moves quickly, and media move toward person-
alized news for monetary and user/rating growth. Native communities appear to
use digital media differently. The use is more about publishing or airing multiple
Native voices by Native people rather than financial gain. As you read through the

examples in this study, you'll see that most Native organizations are nonprofits. Even more profitable papers such as the *Navajo Times* state that their goal is not money. Instead, the *Navajo Times* said it feels rich by providing in-depth community information as it understands that the community is what is culturally important.

Media usage is different in Native communities than in non-Native areas. Older generations rely on word of mouth, newspaper, and radio, while younger Native people go online and on their phones to connect. While oral storytelling is the oldest form of recorded history, ironically, Native journalists believe it is digital media that will extend and resurrect the knowledge of language and detail of storytelling. Generational and media shifts make this time a fruitful ground for research in how digital platforms may be extending Native voices.

Digital media allow for authenticity of Native voices. For instance, concerning the debate about the Washington Redskins name, if non-Native media really want to interview and gain a Native person's perspective, digital media create access to sources. The choice to add an authentic Native perspective and to present nonstereotypical news is really in the hands of those who are reporting. The material is available. The question is whether news organizations want a point of view from a person directly affected by the debate and whether they take the time to educate, reach out, and perhaps accept a different point of view.

Other Native News Organizations Interviewed

Native media are not monolithic. Native news organizations range from one-person newsrooms, reaching hundreds of people in rural areas, to national news distributors that reach hundreds of thousands of people across the country. In-depth analysis of the Native news industry illustrates the importance of truly understanding the individual and the collective American Indian community. While there are overarching views in Indian Country, communities that Native news organizations cover can be vastly different. Because of this diversity within a diverse group, the following Native news organizations were also interviewed for this study.

A national Native radio distributor observed for this study was Native Voice One (NV1), which is part of the Koahnic Broadcast Corporation (KBC). NV1 distributes programs such as *National Native News* and *Native America Calling*. *Native America Calling* is produced at their office in downtown Albuquerque, New Mexico. In front of the building, traffic is heavy, and if you aren't paying attention you will pass the building altogether. Six staff members work in the Albuquerque office. Half of the staff are Native with multiple tribal bloodlines, and half are non-Native. The audience for KBC's program is anyone interested in Native news. The programming for KBC is distributed across Native radio stations in the United States and reaches urban and reservation areas. An estimate of how many people are listening to KBC programs is difficult since many of the listening areas are rural.[22]

Similar to some reservation media, there is a security door in front of the KBC newsroom. A visitor must ring to get in. Once inside the newsroom, the influence of the American Indian community is visible. Hanging on the wall are awards from the Native American Journalists Association (NAJA) as well as a book from the historical Washington, D.C., National Museum of the American Indian. Because of summer holidays and other vacations, some of the interviews for the radio station were later conducted via e-mail or phone.

KNBA

Over the phone, Victoria interviewed a journalist from KBC's nonprofit radio station in Anchorage, Alaska. KNBA-90.3 FM is the first Native urban radio station in the country, and similar to most Native media, it is a nonprofit media outlet. Listeners can receive this station one hundred miles north and south of Anchorage, with approximately fourteen thousand listeners weekly. "This differs from many states due to the fact that Alaska has so much open space between cities."[23]

KNBA's news department is a one-woman newsroom managed by news director Joaqlin Estus. Estus, a member of the Tlingit tribe, said KNBA is utilizing digital media as a virtual beat to aggregate the American Indian online conversations, which include voices from the twenty-six Alaska Native communities. Digital media are especially helpful because the station's coverage takes a different mode of effort from that of journalists who cover nearby towns in the lower forty-eight states.

KNBA's news director recommended contacting the producer of *Heartbeat Alaska* for this study. This broadcast program features Alaska Natives telling stories from their perspective. Jeanie Greene is the solo producer and reporter for this program.[24] She and her husband also are the primary videographers.[25] Greene is Inupiat and from Alaska. She has been a broadcast journalist for more than twenty years. Greene states on her website that she covers everyday stories of people who are Tlingit and Haida, Aleut, Inupiat, Yupik, Athabascan, and Tsimshian.

At the time of the interview, *Heartbeat Alaska* was aired on Coastal Television and published on Greene's web and Facebook pages. Greene did not have rating numbers for her program as it was broadcasted in mostly rural areas, and she said Nielsen ratings numbers are not available for these geographical locations.[26] Perhaps another measurement for *Heartbeat Alaska* is social media. On Facebook, there are currently more than five thousand users following the program. Telling to Greene's digital focus, the entire interview for this study was conducted through Facebook, where Greene constantly is posting news stories and even weather alerts that she feels may not be getting out through mainstream media.

KGUA is a project of the Native Media Resource Center (NMRC).[27] Peggy Berryhill, Muskogee Creek, started the NMRC in 1997 in Gualala, California. She worked in public broadcasting for nearly forty years. The organization consists of three founding members, and the goal is to create content about Native people to promote racial harmony and cross-cultural understanding. NMRC provides content to organizations such as the National Museum of the American Indian, the Corporation for Public Broadcasting, KBC, Northern California Cultural Communications, Inc., and Native American Public Telecommunications (NAPT), Inc.[28]

Berryhill launched KGUA as a branch of NMRC in January 2012. The radio station's audio logo is "where we believe that we all have so much in common." KGUA's primary signal coverage is eighty-five miles and reaches close to one hundred miles along the coast of California from Manchester to Salt Point.[29]

From 2012–13, Berryhill's staff has grown to three part-time volunteers and the vice president of NMRC volunteering to manage the radio station's finances. KGUA is not aware of its exact number of users since it is a rural nonprofit radio station and does not receive official usage ratings. Berryhill reports that her community is around 2,500 residents, and she believes that 25 percent of these listeners discovered her station.[30] The station is seeking more volunteers in order to program in Spanish, English, and Native languages.

KIDE 91.3 FM is the first solar-powered community radio station in California. Unlike the other media in this study, KIDE is a tribal-affiliated radio station. The word *k'ide* is a deer antler that the Hoopa Valley tribe use as a tool or as a decorative ornament.[31] A fourth-grade student in a Hupa language class chose the call letters in 1977. The focus of the radio station is tribal and community news.

The radio station has four full-time staff members and five volunteer hosts that include four sports anchors. The radio station has four main programs connected to health, medicine stories, and language. The station's audience is comprised of about four hundred listeners out of a population of 3,500 people.[32]

KIDE is located in a shopping center behind a food market off of Highway 96 in Hoopa Valley, California. On the radio station's website, the station notes that it is located in an isolated part of Northern California that makes up the Hoopa Valley Indian Reservation. The reservation is situated in a valley between two mountain ranges and the emerald green Trinity River flows through the community. "To reach the community, you must drive along a narrow road that hugs a mountain range 300–600 feet above the Trinity River on the valley floor." The radio station's website explains that Hoopa is a physical gateway, connecting to the Yurok and Karuk tribes. Multicultural villages surround the radio station's listening area.

A staple of Native journalism is Paul DeMain, the executive director and publisher for *News from Indian Country* (*NFIC*). This paper is produced by Indian Country Communications, Inc., and has a sister publication online, Indian Country TV. Indian Country Communications' publications have close to six thousand subscribers and employ four journalists, including the executive director/publisher. Indian Country Communications is an independent, Indian-owned, reservation-based business. The business is located on the Lac Courte Oreilles Ojibwe reservation in Hayward, Wisconsin.[33]

Indian Country Communications has eight stockholders and notes that it is one of the few tribally focused publications that is not owned or politically connected to a tribe. Indian Country Communication has published *NFIC*, the independent Native national newspaper, for more than twenty years. *NFIC* is the oldest national Native newspaper in the United States. The paper publishes fourteen issues a year in print and electronic form.[34] It includes national, cultural, and regional sections and special-interest articles on entertainment.

The *Cherokee Phoenix* was the first newspaper published by American Indians and the first published in Native language. The paper started in 1828 as a symbol of renewal. Originally, the Cherokee Nation started the paper to keep the people united and informed as the government tried to move Cherokees from their land as it was rich with resources. During its inception, and continuing today, the paper serves as the main form of communication for Cherokee people across multiple states in the southeast, allowing for authentic information.[35] The *Cherokee Phoenix*'s circulation is twelve thousand across the United States, and it currently has a staff size of twelve people.[36]

Victoria interviewed journalists from NAPT in 2012. At the start of 2013, the organization changed its name to Vision Maker Media.[37] Vision Maker Media is housed at the University of Nebraska–Lincoln and has twenty-five employees, including student workers, listed on its staff. The organization works with Native television and radio producers to create and distribute educational content across the country to all areas. Vision Maker Media reaches 240 million people through PBS and ten thousand users through social media and e-mail.[38] The distribution company has a strong relationship with tribal nations and Native communities to share Native perspectives across the world.

Mark Trahant is the solo journalist behind *Trahant Reports*, a blog complemented with a Twitter feed. He has more than two thousand followers on Twitter. Trahant notes that anyone may cite the material in his columns located on his blog. Trahant is a blogger, author, and former newspaper editor.[39] He is a member of Idaho's Shoshone-Bannock Tribe and former NAJA president. He posts daily news poems on Twitter and is currently writing a book about austerity. Recently, Trahant appeared on ESPN as an expert to give a Native perspective on the debate about renaming the Washington Redskins.

Last Real Indians (LRI) aims to power a digital rebellion, allowing for Indigenous voices from across the world to be expressed online. Chase Iron Eyes, a Lakota lawyer, was freelancing for Native media when he decided he'd like to provide a platform through which Native voices across the world could be heard. Until 2012, Iron Eyes was writing under the moniker "Last Real Indian." On New Year's of 2012 at midnight, he launched the website LastRealIndians.com. An updated version of the site launched on New Year's Day 2013.

LRI began with four founding writers—identified on its site as renegade scholars. Today the site has grown to dozens of Indigenous contributors across the globe.[40] LRI reports that user hits vary week by week; however, during peak times, it has more than a million hits on Facebook and 80,000 to 120,000 hits on its websites. Founding writer Ruth Hopkins, Sisseton-Wahpeton/Mdewakanton/Hunkpapa, said "during those times we're the most popular Native media site out there."[41] In the future, Iron Eyes wants LRI's website to host live reporting across Native communities, highlighting Indigenous people in the United States, Africa, Europe, Asia, and "whoever is willing to share their stories with us and who has a strong message."[42]

Before this book's research questions are answered, we want to add an additional important point addressing how we approached this analysis. American Indian voices have been marginalized for hundreds of years. This analysis will allow Native voices to breathe as they answer the study's research questions. The concept is that society has consistently shut out or ignored Native voices. This study will not do that. We want the readers to *experience* the unfolding, in-depth conversations with these authentic voices.

The first question this book sought to answer was how the cultural ritual of Native storytelling is connected to reporting by Native media. Three key themes emerged in how Native reporting is similar to Native cultural storytelling. These themes include privacy, detailed meaning, and descriptive language. Each of these elements are tethered to the Native culture and community.

When examining privacy, Native people understand that not all stories are for all people, and the same is true when covering stories in a Native newsroom. Tied to cultural and spiritual beliefs, some stories should not be reported or should be reported at another time.

Concerning digital platforms, Native media will extend some of their news coverage online while other coverage will not be included. Stories such as death are often not detailed within a Native newspaper like the *Navajo Times*. The CEO and publisher of the *Navajo Times*, Tom Arviso, said his staff is continually cognizant that its reporting tends to incorporate the traditional Navajo beliefs. Navajo beliefs impact how the paper covers death, funerals, and domestic violence.

> We are taught that there are certain things that you don't let the public know. Even our own ceremonies . . . There are still things we hold sacred. And, it is because of our Navajo beliefs and culture. We stick with that.[43]

Arviso explained that if a person or family doesn't want the newspaper at the funeral the paper does not attempt to cover this story. He said the paper will try to make arrangements to speak to the families involved with the funeral later, but only if the families accept this idea. There are also times when people stop by the *Navajo Times* with stories about difficulties occurring in their lives. Within Navajo culture, ceremonies are held for people having hard times. Thus, even if the event is covered, that portion of the story will not be reported. "We'll leave it out of the story. Even though it is an important part. There are certain things we still respect. I think that is another one of our strengths."[44]

Senior *Navajo Times* reporter Marley Shebala noted the role of these healing ceremonies. She said the whole Navajo community is involved, again, because one person's behavior can have a far-reaching effect on a lot of people. Each ceremony includes specific ways through which the victim and the perpetrator are viewed. Each individual is expected to speak openly about what has happened. Shebala compared it to the "western way" of talking about a problem: talking about it "releases it." "We always understood that that is part of our healing . . . and it is like oh, what a relief. I finally told everyone what I did or oh, what a relief to know everyone knows why I am acting ill or suffering."[45]

Ceremonies allow for the understanding of what was done wrong so that the community knows how to pray for all involved. The community understands that when topics are addressed in ceremony they does not need to be dealt with again in the press. A ceremony allows for the airing out of information in a supportive environment versus the press.

Unlike mainstream media, Native media focus more on the privacy of the collective community. However, concerning sourcing, if a person is a public official, Native journalists note the official is then serving the community and should be covered. The officials have chosen to put themselves and their families into the public eye.[46]

Sourcing is important in tight communities. Shebala said public officials say to her that in the Navajo way she is their little sister, big sister, mother, or grandmother. She said officials often ask why she is reporting negative news.

> And I tell them I was taught a long time ago when each of the clans would come together that there would be a person that would tell what was going on in the community. So the community knew what was going on. . . . when there was something good, they were happy and everyone shared in happy. If there was something not good, everyone shared in that. They didn't shy away from talking about sexual deviancy and I said, everything was open and even the leadership—especially leadership.[47]

The history of the clans and their openness support Shebala's feelings that public officials, as well as tribal meetings, should be open for discussion by the press and community. Historically, she said, officials don't "hide" in meetings when something serious happened. Noting that even if there were serious matters such as sexual deviancy, when the tribe still had organized clans, it would have a person who served as a reporter to speak openly with officials. Official information was then spread throughout the tribe.

Detailed Meaning Tied to Beliefs

The reporting by the Native press also is different from the mainstream press in how reporters construct detailed stories. Storytelling within the Native community is a loaded word and has a complex connotation. Meaning goes beyond a definition and includes the Creator, history, and lessons on how to live in the present and future.

> There's different types of stories that people talk about. The beginning of the Navajo life, all the way through changing woman to birth of changing woman to white shell woman, and the different worlds we have lived in. I think we are going into our fifth world. The different ceremonies, they all have significant meaning to it. How it started, the purpose of the ceremony, and the end results of those ceremonies is of course the well-being of the patient.[48]

This meaning-making matches the overall Native culture perfectly with journalism: crafting narrative in a manner to understand a story *and* a phenomenon. Native news masters a main element within journalism and that is telling stories that connect to life and communities. "There is more emotion (in covering Native stories). There is more of a human element—attachment to the animals and vice versa. So when we have a problem like with what is going on with the horses, there is an abuse there."[49] Details are important in stories, such as abuse, because these stories reflect a larger cultural story. For example, discussing roaming horses not receiving enough water is more than an investigative story in the newspaper. The abuse reflects how Navajo lives might be changed in the future because the land and animals are lacking essential survival resources. "In the Navajo culture, you aren't supposed to do that. If you have horses running wild and starving and they are getting all chewed up and dying, that is really disrespectful to them and ultimately it will come back and hurt us as a people."[50] The tragedy surrounding horses may appear as a sad isolated story from a mainstream media perspective. However, the story is tied to violations of Native beliefs. Abuse is not just a violation of law but has a greater effect on the overall community and therefore the world.

Bill Donovan, a non-Native reporter from Kentucky who freelances for the mainstream local paper and has worked for the *Navajo Times* off and on since the 1970s, explained the differences when he wrote a story for the *Navajo Times* versus the *Gallup Independent*.

I can't get the people at the *Gallup Independent* to understand. A lot of time when I write a story for the *Independent,* they rework it. They say it is not in the traditional journalism mode. But when I write a story for the *Navajo Times,* it is better with more detail . . . you see me write a story for the *Independent* and the newspaper here on the same subject, it is sometimes different because of that.[51]

Reporting from the perspectives of different communities took some research by Donovan. In 1968, Donovan was a police reporter covering civil rights at a mainstream paper in Kentucky and met a Navajo man he called by his last name, Triplett. Triplett was working in the police department and also was covering civil rights issues. The Navajo man told Donovan to "go cover the Navajos because no one else is."[52] Donovan said that he didn't know anything about the Navajo community.

Triplett had what Donovan called a Native sense of humor. Scholars have cited Native humor as essentially teasing of an outside group about Native culture because there is such a lack of understanding about it.[53]

When I went and told him I got the job, he said you realize Navajos don't speak English. He started speaking Navajo and I said I'm never going to understand that. . . . Don't worry because all Navajos know sign language. So I bought a book . . . and all the way on the drive here I was studying that book trying to learn sign language. I have yet to find one Navajo who knows sign language. So shows you how naïve I was here.[54]

This good-humored teasing was memorable to the Navajo staff because more than one *Navajo Times* reporter mentioned that Victoria must hear this story before she left. The story had been passed down from staff generation to staff generation and now to her.

Radio station manager for the California Hoopa Valley tribal radio, KIDE, Joseph Orozco said he believes Native media are so important he wishes the press would have been established as a "sovereign right" in the treaties with the U.S. government. Orozco noted that he understands why it wasn't in the treaties because at that time there wasn't media, as we know it, much less digital media. "We didn't have television, radio, and all that . . . if it was a sovereign right and if the federal government had a mandate to sensitize media in Indian Country—where they have a radio station or just a newspaper or both—it would make media a viable career choice."[55]

Descriptive Language, Oral and Written

Native journalists noted that digital media are changing the ritual of storytelling by honoring the details that reside in Native storytelling. For instance, the Navajo language is very descriptive. "I'll have editors and it depends if they know Navajo language or not. They'll say, oh, your stories are too detailed and I say, I guess that is the Navajo in me coming out. They'll look at me sideways and say, what? I say, inside joke."[56]

Description beyond the written word engenders an attempt to include meaning in reporting. One newspaper reporter said the use of video along with her story helps to express a deeper meaning.[57]

When asking newspaper employees about writing in a language, Navajo, that lends itself to compelling oral storytelling, one older newspaper employee said he did not know how to write down the words in which he spoke. To him and others, Navajo is an oral language designed to describe and explain.[58] One example of not being able to write down a spoken word is the paper's name itself; the Navajo language translates the name of the newspaper into a "newspaper that gossips." "When you talk about it in Navajo there is no other way that we'd translate. It is just like that—the newspaper that gossips, that talks about other people and things. In a way it can be looked at as a good thing or looked at as a negative thing."[59]

Native journalists hope that digital media may help bridge the gap between the oral and written Navajo word—including between those Navajos who live on and off the reservation. The only senior reporter at the *Navajo Times* would like the paper to be able to digitally record the Navajo language and provide it as an option next to the online news stories. "You click on a button and it'll pop up into the Navajo language and you click on another button and you'll hear it in Navajo—being read to you because a lot of our elders they speak Navajo, but they don't read it."[60]

Beyond the oral and written word, the *Navajo Times* is attempting to create a platform for those with access on the reservation and for those in mobile areas. The tradition of language may be changing depending on where American Indians live. *Navajo Times* human resource manager Franklin Yazzie said his children, who live in a city, have a different need for information compared to his stepchildren on the reservation.

> They have their jobs and they are doing well versus my stepdaughters that's income level are not as high but they know more of the Navajo language and culture versus

my own children. My son says I'd rather be out here earning some decent wages. He has a home. Runs his own business. He says I don't have to know the language. I don't have to know the traditions as long as I get a paycheck every week. Then, versus over here, my stepdaughter she says I'd rather take care of the livestock—sheep being sacred to the Navajo people. She always makes ends meet somehow. She has a part-time job. It has its checks and balances.[61]

So that it can reach all Navajos, the *Navajo Times* provides content in a weekly subscription electronic edition launched last year as well as on its website, mobile application, Facebook page, and in the traditional hard copy of the paper. The different platforms allow for Navajos, no matter their access, to be able to connect with the community coverage.

We are trying to use all [digital platforms] to draw back to our print. We are hoping our e-edition is going to kick off and bring extra funding to our paper. The way I really see it going is because of our location and our lack of infrastructure on the Navajo Nation our print edition is going to continue to be more appreciated and more needed for our local Navajo people. However, we are trying to push further out. We have 320,000 Navajos. The majority of those are eighteen and under, but those are going to be the ones that start utilizing computers a lot more. So in time we are hoping it is going to kick up our e-edition subscriptions because again those are going to be the ones living out in the metropolitan areas—Phoenix, Albuquerque, Denver—beyond the boundaries we are not going to be able to deliver the paper.[62]

As Native media outlets look to the future, it is the Native culture that still guides its media decisions. Stories are written and told in a detailed and descriptive manner. While this culture is rooted in history, ironically it is the *new* media platforms that allow a once primarily oral group to express its stories through media. Audio, video, social media, and print provide a fruitful multimedia platform through which Native people can produce detailed stories and share them across the world.

Native News Reach

This book's second research question sought to examine how digital media are changing the routine of reporting on Native issues. No research exists that specifically discusses the norms and routines of American Indian media. Yet Indigenous people were the first to live on the land that now houses one of the most powerful media systems in the world. Observations from this study, as well as journalist interviews, provide a starting point for understanding Native norms and routines. This new knowledge can help facilitate the understanding of how digital platforms may be impacting them. The reach of Native news is changing with digital platforms, and Native journalists have their own routines in deciding what sources are credible online.

The most popular way for American Indians to receive news is by word of mouth, radio, and/or newspaper. The more rural the area in which a Native person lives the more likely he/she relies on newspaper and/or radio; however, mobile technology and the Internet are changing how all Natives receive news.[63]

> Our goal is to reach everyone . . . whether they are living in a rural community without access to the Internet or whether they have every device you can imagine. That was actually one of the reasons we started the radio show. We found that many of people who live in areas that don't have Internet connection, they listen to the radio so we felt like that was a very cost-effective way to reach a huge audience of people that we were never going to reach through our website.[64]

Digital media are changing the role of Native reporting by redefining how reporters produce and distribute content. Digital platform audiences have shorter attention spans and require shorter and more frequent updates.[65] The Native news process is no longer a waiting game for receiving or distributing information. The Internet allows Native news organizations to distribute information across multiple platforms beyond the newspaper's press run or radio air time.

American Indian journalists understand their community and that there is a divide, but the degree of the divide is changing. Seventy percent of those who are Native live outside the reservation, which means they may have greater access to the Internet and access to digital forms of media.[66] Meanwhile, the growth of mobile technology allows for residents on the reservation to rely not only on its infrastructure for Internet and wireless capabilities, but to be able to log on where cell phone towers are available.

Many Native people live in rural locations. This often means infrastructures are not as capable of hosting Internet service. The foundation for many Native communities is one that supports newspaper and radio media systems.[67]

> On the reservation itself not too many people have computers. Both radio and the newspaper are the information that is sent out to other people and received. I have a brother who lives out in White Corn. He lives maybe thirty miles from the trading post. He says every Thursday morning he gets his paper and at the same time he has his radio.[68]

Radio

NV1 is a national radio company that distributes KBC's live call-in, news, and music programs. The turnaround time for completely preproduced programs is typically two weeks. "If we want to replace a show, if something happens on Monday, we can replace it on Friday. So we are not as fast as mainstream in that sense."[69]

KBC owns NV1. The broadcast corporation's office in downtown Albuquerque, New Mexico, is where NV1 produces most programs.[70] KBC also owns the only American Indian owned-and-operated radio station in an urban environment—KNBA in Anchorage, Alaska.

Using Digital Platforms for Content and Sourcing

Joaqlin Estus is the news director at KBC's KNBA and the only employee in the news department. Estus said she had to adjust to working in a one-person newsroom. Earlier she'd worked at Minnesota Public Radio and at stations where there were editors and other reporters she collaborated with on stories. At MPR, she also had a station vehicle that she could use to cover stories.

In comparison to Minnesota, if Estus wants to report on an Alaskan village outside of Anchorage she gathers her information by phone or online. She said some Alaska reporters take commercial flights to cover sources, but because of the financial limitations of travel she spends hours a day looking for stories on the Internet. She said this is a change from when she first started working in radio and received most information by phone or fax. Now she said she can get court rulings, reports, and previous news stories—a year's worth of information—in minutes online versus just a two- to three-page fax.

She has her own routine in how she manages information from social media. If the information is provided by a public information source she will report on it, treating it as if she received that information through more traditional routes such as e-mail or phone. However, if information is in the form of a personal social media post or Tweet she will not include this information on the radio.

> I think it is unethical of course to copy other people's reporting. If I read something like Alaska Dispatch, which is an online news source, I'd use for story ideas. We go to them for a lot of good stories. I always go back to the original source and quote the document that they might have also used, or I'd interview the people that they may talk with and basically write my own story. Now the only thing I actually take off the Internet is the Associated Press or from the Alaska Public Radio Network.[71]

Estus, the sole content gatekeeper in the newsroom, struggles when deciding what stories to cover. She said she is constantly checking the rundown of content she puts on air because she doesn't want it to be her own news agenda. She also said she had to come to grips with covering stories that other Alaska radio journalists would also report within her network. Her station is a part of the Alaska Public Radio Network, and she said she would be concerned when she would cover stories and there would be other reporters from the same network present at the scene. Then, she realized being Native meant she had a different concept of covering news:

> My perspective as an Alaska Native is completely different than that as a non-Native. My mission is different so if I go to a statewide event, like suppose I go to a candidate's forum and all kinds of reporters are there and they are all asking the candidates all these types of questions, everything from oil and gas developments to revenues to state agencies and that sort of thing. Well, I will listen to everything they say and if I ask questions, it'll be related to Alaska Natives so I think no matter what the event I'm pulling out something different than the other reporters are. So I try to avoid duplicative efforts, but if it happens, I'm OK with it.[72]

One salient difference between Native and mainstream coverage is story selection. For example, Alaska Natives live mostly in rural areas and depend on food gathered from the land and water. Changes with the climate influence the decreasing food supply, which is a huge part of the rural economy. In regional hubs, maybe 60 to 70 percent of residents gather food from the wild versus other villages where 90 percent of the community gets food from the wild. Estus said there's much more to it, though, than just putting food on the table. "I think it's a justifiable source of pride to people who have the expertise to hunt, fish, and gather enough food not only for themselves but for their extended family and community. Respect for the animals and for nature is important. And getting food brings with it an obligation to share with others. Those values are deeply embedded in Alaska Natives cultures." She says other coverage often focuses on subsistence as a fish and game management issue rather than mainstay of Alaska Native cultures.

Again, this is another example of the circle of life and connection to all things in nature that culturally isn't as prevalent in most non-Native's daily lives. Estus also says climate change in Alaska affects Native people's live. In the Arctic, where the permafrost is melting and the infrastructure is lacking, the villages don't have running water, piped water, and/or flushable toilets. Instead, the villages contain a central location from which residents can haul water to their homes. The water costs money, though, so people often collect rainwater and haul water or ice from rivers and lakes. This causes health problems. One in four babies in villages in southwest Alaska without indoor plumbing are hospitalized for respiratory infections, Estus reported. Estus explains that this is a lifestyle that some mainstream news organizations may have a hard time understanding and consequently accurately reporting about.[73]

Natives are more likely to see and report on issues differently because, to some degree, they live in the culture on which they are reporting. Whether in Alaska or in the lower forty-eight states, Indian Country comprehends the diversity contained in these communities. American Indians digest the range of lifestyle differences between Natives in all areas.

Newspapers

Meanwhile, Native newspapers publish information at a different pace than KNBA's daily news updates. Most tribal newspapers typically print only once a month, while some are biweekly.[74] Independent Native newspapers such as the *Navajo Times* print weekly. The *Navajo Times* at one time attempted to produce a daily product, but it wasn't financially feasible.[75]

Unlike mainstream news organizations, print is still the most popular way to receive information in all Native communities. Most Native reporters work at Native newspapers because it is a connection to their community and their people.

> To me, it's like you have *Navajo Times* in the Native American media and it is like the equivalent of the *New York Times* in a sense. I never had the desire to going to *New York Times* or *Washington Post* or any major papers. Some journalism students do, they have that ambition. But to me it was like I will go to the *Navajo Times*. I think that is where I can do the best, as far as I am concerned.[76]

In 2013, the NAJA included Native journalists in traditional and emerging news media. The organization said that, unlike the mainstream press, the numbers appear steady for Native print journalists. The organization has 230 members, with most members working for tribal print media. The NAJA feels the print model seems to work well for many Native audiences. "Publication costs are often picked up by individual tribes, making it easier for them to survive, even in a digital age."[77]

The NAJA noted that many of its members, in addition to producing printed news content, also shared messages via social media sites. The NAJA has its own Facebook group on which many post questions, news, and employment needs. The organization explained that social media make it convenient for Native journalists as they can share their messages in a timely manner. This allows them the same freedom as other online formats without an associated cost.[78]

For non-Natives, it is important to understand how Native news consumers read the newspaper. While on the reservation, Victoria personally witnessed readers getting up at the crack of dawn to get their *Navajo Times*. The reading of the paper appeared to be a ritual much like morning coffee. Traditionally, families see the paper as a record extending history. From their experiences, Native journalists explained the paper isn't skimmed for headlines, but instead read and reread. One paper is shared across a family, making it hard to calculate the exact number of Native readers.

> People will buy the paper and they take it home and it is shared with seven or eight other people in the family. It doesn't just sit there on the counter. It's read over and over for like a whole month. Most newspapers you can read in ten to fifteen minutes. That is it and they are done, but our newspaper has a lot longer life.[79]

The weekly *Navajo Times* is hefty, lending it to being read more than once. The paper includes three sections, and each section is ten to twelve pages in length, containing detailed community stories. The paper appears much thicker than mainstream dailies or even weekly papers, as they are shrinking with economic downsizing.

Digital Divide and Convergence

A generational technology divide exists in Indian Country.[80] While some reporters feel the Native press is behind ten to twenty years, the younger generation appears to want Native news faster than its traditional form can provide. Native reporters are grappling with how to provide news to young and/or urban American Indians, while respecting those who live where American Indian culture is thriving: on the reservation.

> How do you get it to go towards an audience that isn't technologically there yet? You go out onto the reservation and you got homes that still don't have electricity at this time and age. Don't have running water. How are they going to do that? Yeah, they can use their phone, but our Grandpa and Grandma wouldn't be interested in using a touch screen to look at news. They are so used to newspapers.[81]

Even with limited access on the reservation, the Native press is pushing to publish online, including social media. From what *Navajo Times* reporter Noel Lyn Smith experienced, Indian Country appears to use social media like Facebook because of its collective quality, almost like community members having a conversation online.[82] However, it is the younger generation and the 70 percent of Natives who live off the reservation who are connecting.[83]

While community respect remains for older generations and/or those living on the reservation, Native news outlets are trying to balance providing information in the traditional ways and through digital media. With so many Natives living off the reservation, urban areas provide opportunities to connect. Many Native newspapers are increasing their accessibility through mobile applications, electronic editions, and news websites.[84]

To provide information faster to the community, in 2011 the *Navajo Times* started posting daily videos to its website, which it started in 1999. With the daily videos to the web, a newspaper reporter functions more like a news anchor, recording five-minute headline news through YouTube then uploading. The newspaper's editor writes the news script for the reporter to read. Because of work schedules, the paper's editor, who reports to work earlier than the reporters, also records these headline stories. The news report airs on KYAT, an all-Navajo-language radio channel in Gallup, New Mexico.

Unlike mainstream newspapers, the editor at the *Navajo Times* writes the headline stories for radio and the web. At the time of Victoria's visit, Duane Beyal was the editor of the paper and wrote the morning updates. He recorded them live at 8:30 a.m. so that they could rebroadcast two more times that day.[85] Beyal said he gets facts for these headlines from several sources. The paper uses the Associated Press wires, checks the in-coming mail containing press releases, and goes through e-mail. However, the *Navajo Times* prefers original stories that the paper's journalists discover.

Technology and Writing

The book's third research question examined how digital media are changing Native reporter's news-coverage routines. Beyond narratives and writing, how Native news organizations are distributing news is also changing. KBC provides Native programs on the Internet and distributes programs for Native radio stations across the country. The organization said that with the development of new technology it witnessed a growth in podcasting. KBC uses the Internet to upload programs so that its affiliates can download them anywhere in the country. "The way we are distributing things is fast and the way they [the affiliates] are sending information, their stories, is fast."[86]

The *Navajo Times* reported its audience as 80 percent print and 20 percent online. The paper said new technology allows the press to give its take on a story faster.[87] For example, if a story breaks after the weekly paper's distribution, technology gives the paper an opportunity to cover the story before waiting another week to print.

> The print edition is limited in how far it can reach people, but with our online presence we are able to have everybody has access to it, if they want it. . . . That way if something happens up in Fort Hall, Idaho, with the Sho-Ban and they put it on their website . . . I'm able to know what's happening there and vice versa so it's really a good thing. It is a positive thing.[88]

The oldest Native paper in the United States, the *Cherokee Phoenix*, sees the news the paper is publishing in traditional forms mushrooming across digital media. The executive editor for the paper described Cherokee communities as tightly knit. Because of this, he said, when the paper publishes a story he sees feedback or references across the paper's multiple digital platforms.

> If we publish a story one day on our website, people talk about it and then look for it in the paper. Or, they will listen to it on our radio show or look for it on our Facebook page. So we get a lot of people kind of cross-referencing and going back and forth to our different platforms, and it creates a broad community conversation about it.[89]

Much like mainstream media, Indian Country Communications executive director Paul DeMain said he sees mobile technology, video, and the element of live broadcasts as the future for Native media. He said he believes these news-coverage components will be how Native news organizations will continue to thrive through digital changes. Paul DeMain runs *News from Indian Country* and Indian Country TV and is the former president of the NAJA. He noted that his news organization uses YouTube to distribute his daily headlines on its website, on Facebook, and through e-mail. He said YouTube is easily visible on mobile phones and provides an accessible live stream. DeMain said he understood that it was important that he have video, but also an effective way to distribute it. Two years ago, DeMain decided that Indian Country Communications needed to include video. He said the communication organization bought Indian Country TV since publishing for Indian Country is the staple of his organization's newspaper and television product.[90]

Technology has changed the writing style for one American Indian journalist, a former editor of the *Navajo Times*. Mark Trahant was working in mainstream media when he lost his job in 2009.[91] Trahant's job loss opened a new door. The soon to be 2013/14 Atwood Chair at the University of Alaska–Anchorage was the first Native news blogger. On *Trahant Reports*, he describes himself as a writer and "Twitter poet."

The primary way Trahant sees media changing through technology is the "idea of the written word. It is just another way to tell a story and in this case trying to get a story down to 140 characters."[92] When describing the difference from writing in a longer newspaper print format to covering stories in 140 characters online, he said the skill takes practice and he has been practicing since 2009. "I think writing is like anything else. The more you do it, the more you practice, the easier it gets. It is sort of like exercise for the brain."[93]

With the constantly evolving new media, Trahant noted writers must remember context when reporting in these digital platforms. At the time of the interview, he said he tried to take advantage of the new tools to get the key stories across without losing the circumstances around the story. On his blog, he has news stories such as "How Did Native Americans Impact the 2012 Election?"[94] Trahant thinks story coverage is twofold: the day-to-day account of what is happening and the larger thematic narrative, with the latter being the one to which journalists need to give detailed attention.

Trahant said he has a larger function for how he uses digital media. He is attempting to use the new media platform to change the way the Native community thinks about existing narratives. His work and Twitter poems can be found on both Twitter and Facebook.

> An example of one [the big story] I've been trying to change myself is Indian health. It is very difficult because the previous story is so deep in our psyche . . . the story has been for the past fifteen years about the Indian Health Service and its problem, its shortcomings, and its underfunding.[95]

Trahant said instead of focusing on the negative side of Indian health he is attempting to shift this story to the systems that seem to work in Indian Country, noting that this positive take is a completely different narrative from the past.

Access

Technology assists with covering quickly developing stories in the Navajo community. However, *Navajo Times* head photographer Paul Natonabah detailed the legwork the paper has gone to in the past to receive access to breaking news. One story was prominent in his mind. When Victoria interviewed the serious, yet kind Natonabah and, in contrast, carefree press operator Leonard Sylvan separately, they both recounted the story's facts in the same manner, a story that is still today on the *New York Times*'s website even though it occurred in 1984.[96]

A large B-52 crashed in Kayenta, Arizona, 134 miles from Window Rock in October 1984. The crash happened at night, and so Natonabah, Sylvan, and now blogger Mark Trahant (who was the *Navajo Times* editor at the time) all went to cover the breaking news. The three drove to the site in Natonabah's GTO.

The *Navajo Times* journalists wanted to find the crash site because they felt it was especially newsworthy, since B-52s flew frequently from Utah to Phoenix. The officials wouldn't tell the journalists the location. Apparently, the plane had flown low and crashed, bursting into flames. "Some people tried to jump off, parachute, but it didn't open or something. We drove down the road because everybody heard about it. All this news media."[97]

The journalists stopped at a police station to discover the location. They noticed a non-Native news organization coming toward them to share information.

> Then we saw a headlight come closer, closer. Here was that KOB-TV from Farmington. They said, they won't let you. It is police blocked. . . . This man, he looks like Navajo. To me. He looked like cameraman. Sure enough police were parked down there. You could see their lights. It was still dark. He talked in Navajo to me: [Natonabah translated when telling the story] Where are you guys going? [spoken in Navajo]. Going home. Where are you guys from? In Navajo, I said we just coming from a school dance and we are going home. Okay. We passed the police line. That's a long story, you know.[98]

The journalists hiked to the top of the mesa. There were military police and a large helicopter circling. Natonabah had his camera and took pictures.

> Mark was thinking. He said quickly, rewind that film. I did that and gave it to him. This was in winter and so it was cold and we wear a jacket. So he put the film and he hid it in his big jacket. We walk up steep. Mark was trying to climb up the rock and he slip and slide down. He had some scrapes. We went up there and then the military guy says, stop! We know who you guys are. Now go back. He says, oh by the way, you a photographer? Give me your film, he says to me. I'm pretending unwinding. I took it out and let them have it.[99]

Trahant wrote the breaking news story as Natonabah developed the film. The Associated Press wanted the B-52 crash story quickly. The journalists made some prints and rushed them to the airport to get them to Phoenix. "The next day it was in the daily paper. That was one of the highlights of my career."[100]

Natonabah's crash story illustrates the lengths the *Navajo Times* staff has gone to in the past to cover breaking news. Today, the "work" of covering breaking news has changed with digital media. While officials may not support a newsroom having access to a breaking news site, mobile phones and other digital elements provide a different sort of access to stories. If journalists or news consumers witness a story, they can push the boundaries of access and release information digitally. Hiking to the tops of mesas doesn't need to occur as frequently for these journalists anymore.

Community Coverage

Along with covering developing stories, community journalism is a staple of the *Navajo Times*. Native news organizations, much like other diverse media, cover their community the mainstream press ignores or misunderstands. Native news organizations focus on their minority audience and cover stories relevant to their audiences, often with a greater emphasis on community. Senior reporter Marley Shebala, who reflects an inquisitive, fiery reporter flare, finds her definition of community is different from mainstream reporters.

> You don't have a lot of community journalists because they really aren't a part of the community. . . . I was talking to this Washington, D.C., reporter and she said she had been in D.C. for ten years and that was really long for her, and I says that is good then you have really made a home there and that's your community. I'm sure you built sources. She said, well, she says, I don't know if I have built sources, but I do know it is not home, she says, because she really didn't know her neighbors in that sense.[101]

Shebala said she wouldn't change reporting for her community on the reservation because she has the history and the knowledge that the community truly needs for accurate reporting. However, that doesn't mean that reporting on such a tight-knit community is easy. Shebala said it can be tough being so connected to the community when it comes to investigative reporting. She said she has to ask hard questions about people and families that she is culturally connected to and has known for a long time.

As a Navajo, she said she is able to get more in-depth coverage of her community because she is on the same cultural level as the individuals on whom she reports.

> Compared to the *Gallup Independent, Farmington Daily Times*, they have writers and reporters who go out and talk to people and come back, but because they are not Native they don't see the same type of feedback we do. So again it is something very unique that we have available to our readers.[102]

Some Native journalists said there is also a difference between mainstream and Native norms and routines as mainstream media are more structured than Native news.

> I think that non-Native media covers stories in a much more strict way. Native media, however, covers media in a really relaxed way. For instance we [*NFIC*/Indian Country TV] went and did some coverage of the Nagaajiwanaang [Fond du Lac] language camp. We had so much fun with all the activities from the canoe races to the talent show that I forgot I wasn't on vacation.[103]

In the *Navajo Times* newsroom, the feeling is more relaxed than in mainstream news organizations. In contrast to mainstream newsrooms, Native music, conversation, and laughter replaces droning police scanners. Through observation, the newsroom felt more like a community where senior reporters like Marley Shebala groomed younger reporters such as Noel Lyn Smith. When specifically discussing news stories, the focus was more on how to tell the story. At times there would be a collective discussion between the more senior and younger reporters.

For several people in the newsroom, the paper meant more than a job. Several journalists discussed how they remembered touring the paper as a child. They also told stories of their families sending them to the trading post on Thursday mornings to pick up the *Navajo Times*. The paper was a connection not only to current events, but to a community and culture.

Witnessing Shebala during a tribal council budget and finance meeting illustrated her connection to the community. The council debated what to do about issues such as water availability. During this meeting, a proposal was on the table for the Navajo-Hopi Little Colorado River Water settlement; the committee called Shebala by her first name when she asked questions. Other meeting attendees, primarily those who were not a part of the Navajo community, such as non-Native journalists and a federal government representative, the council addressed formally by their last names.

A difference between Native and mainstream media was also clear during the tribal council meeting in terms of commitment to coverage. When the tribal council wanted to meet privately without noncouncil in the room, the mainstream press reporter appeared stressed, tired, and ready to get the news and leave, possibly battling a daily news deadline. In contrast, Shebala, with her strong connection and emphasis on total community coverage, stayed the entire meeting and talked to the officials afterward. Shebala said she often goes up after meetings and asks for all the paperwork she can get. She'll take the large binder, containing hundreds of pages of documents, back to the newspaper, copy, and return them. She said if she doesn't get these official documents during the official meetings she may never see the paperwork, and it could take months just to get a fraction of that material.

Conclusion

This chapter examined how digital media are changing the routine of reporting on Native issues. This is the first research specifically discussing the norms and routines of American Indian media. The new digital emerging platforms are changing how journalists cover stories for the Native press. Similar to the mainstream, journalists have to produce stories faster and in a shorter format; however, unlike the mainstream, Native news organizations will still take the time to advance these stories with the cultural descriptive detail online. To enhance this detail, digital media allow Native news organizations to reach out to Indigenous people across the world to provide a complete cultural community story. Multimedia provide Native news organizations the ability to surround print news with elements such as audio, video, and social media interactivity, resulting in news coverage depth that mirrors Native language.

The routine that honors the time and attention needed to craft a detailed, representative, and accurate news story is the same routine Shebala respects in her multimedia journalist role. During the tribal council meeting, Shebala freely roamed taking digital pictures for the paper, checking and double-checking her pictures to make sure that she photographed the correct person and in the correct manner. She said she didn't want to take a picture that would add false meaning to her story because the person was in midsentence discussing another matter.

In a juxtaposition to technology with the digital pictures Shebala took, parts of the reservation have a lack of cell phone service, and this included where the tribal committee meeting took place. Reporters were aware that if they sat in the back row in the middle of the room and put their phone in the middle of the window they might get service. While advances in digital media are accelerating the production of Native stories, the culture of storytelling in Native communities engenders caution and precision. The use of photography, visuals, audio, and an array of digital platforms to distribute these stories allows Native communities, like many others at this time, to hurdle some invisibility barriers; but that technology is not overwhelming the journalists or dictating the story, as is the case in some mainstream outlets.

CHAPTER 4

Looking Forward

This book's fourth research question examined how digital media usage breaks down barriers between mainstream and Native media to advance the visibility of American Indian communities. To address what more can be done to advance the visibility and positive portrayals of American Indians through digital media, it is important to remember why Native journalists feel stereotypes continue to reoccur. Barriers between mainstream media and Native journalists include lack of knowledge and exposure and a vast geographical coverage area.

Multiple Native journalists cited mainstream coverage as sustaining American Indian stereotypes.[1] The non-Native press tend to leave out community. Mainstream media cover Indian Country mainly during times of conflict and do not include Native people as part of their daily news beats.

Bryan Pollard, executive editor of the *Cherokee Phoenix*, said the main step that mainstream media can make is to stop using stereotypes in all their forms, overt and inferential. He said mascots, stereotypes, epithets, and zoo and frozen-in-time stories all need to be eradicated. "It is almost a no brainer. It is hard to believe we are even still talking about it."

Many people know enough about it to know it is not pretty. So when you have that type of blanket denial and that type of desensitivity the only thing that rises through the service is stereotypes, the PowWows and all that stuff. . . . I was watching a news show the other night and they referred to the meeting of some of the congressional leaders as a PowWow. I was, like you know, that just rolled off the person's tongue like it was nothing there—there was no consideration to Native people.[2]

Stereotypical Coverage

Native journalists felt that some of the mainstream media stereotypical coverage was not necessarily intentional, but instead an absence of interest in the Native community.[3] Native journalists said they believe non-Native people do not think of Native journalism existing unless it is connected to stories that address non-Native people's history.[4] In contrast, the Native perspective is not addressed in history. Therefore, a Native's views of the past, the present, and the future are not part of the non-Native narrative and educational curriculum.

Recently, in some Native communities, mainstream media expanded their news coverage.

Anchorage mainstream media has finally caught on to the fact that Alaska is more than the urban cities. Most of Alaska is rural, and until my program, *Heartbeat Alaska*, this giant segment of Alaska was not considered worthy of mainstream news media. Today, you will see the news trying to catch up to what I've been covering for twenty-two years.[5]

Before this expansion, mainstream media frequently assumed that all American Indians had the same thoughts and feelings and actions across the hundreds of tribes.

A Native organization that employs both Native and non-Native workers said its news company's goal is opposite of the mainstream press when it comes to Native voices. Instead of providing the same stereotypical script, Koahnic Broadcast Corporation (KBC) attempts to get out as many Native voices as possible. This distribution allows for those tuning in on air and/or online to hear thoughts and feelings from the overall Native community. Hearing the diversity within American Indian communities helps eliminate the prominent stereotypical script. "Our work here at Koahnic Broadcast stations is to be the leader to get the Native voice heard. Everything we do focus on getting their voices out and their stories heard. I think in mainstream media, especially when I was in television news, that's not the purpose."[6]

Unlike how the mainstream media often show American Indians, not all tribes or persons are the same. Will Kie, associate producer for KBC's *Native America Calling*, provided a different view from the stereotypes that the media often perpetuate.

> I have been honest with the people here; I grew up in popular culture. I had a connection to my Native people and my community.... Growing up in the eighties, I grew up on Guns-N-Roses. I knew about Metallica.... I didn't listen to PowWow music. I couldn't tell you which drum group or which style what, so I don't know that part.[7]

He said he is a country and a rock fan, and another person in his company's specialty is traditional PowWow music.

Connecting with Native Communities beyond Conflict Coverage

The lack of interest in the community perhaps is the reason why mainstream media cover the Native community only when it views a viable story such as one that contains conflict or drama. KGUA general manager, Peggy Berryhill, said that she recently viewed a television news report about the Pine Ridge reservation, and the reporter did not research the area she was reporting on and instead focused her story on victimization.

> There was a really popular news anchor. A well-known national news anchor who went to a reservation and did her story. It left people in tears, but it was once again these poor victims and here are a couple kids that are struggling, you know? And we are going to hope for the best for them, but really did nothing to help understand the so-called plight.[8]

Berryhill said, instead, the mainstream press should have taken the time to understand the history of the reservation, examining the deeper contextual issues. In contrast, she felt the news organizations picked a few young children to interview and didn't explain the actual progress on the reservation. Berryhill feels it is important for outside journalists to spend time in Native country, not just when conflict occurs. Just as important, Native people need to continue to cover Native stories so that authentic voices are heard within the press.

To have a factually and contextually accurate news story, a journalist must spend time and talk to those in American Indian communities.[9] American Indian reporters covering tribal stories know the "movers and shakers" within their own tribes, essentially the credible perceived sources to interview. For a Native reporter who is a community outsider, it can take months to build trust to cover a story. Former Native American Journalists Association (NAJA) executive director Jeff Harjo discussed his process of covering the Kickapoo tribe in Oklahoma. He said it took him approximately six months to gain the trust of the tribe, by showing up at every news event with a camera.[10] Fortunately in terms of this study, Victoria knew gatekeepers for many of the interviews who carefully conducted introductions.

Senior reporter Marley Shebala said the way to change stereotypical representations in traditional and digital media is for non-Native organizations to integrate this community within its beat system. She said there is no reason why a person living in the United States should not visit a reservation. She said Indigenous people were the first communities here, and journalists should visit and cover them—not just when a controversial or cultural event occurs but instead as part of their daily news routine.

> Go out there and cover them, and don't just cover them when something controversial happens: the government is being overthrown, someone commits suicide, or domestic violence. Because you are also not doing fair and balanced coverage of that community, and you wonder why they don't want to talk to you. But, if you are out there from the beginning covering those events—police Olympics, their little races, and not just cultural events either, school events, anything that goes on in that community. When something big happens in that community, they are going to call you. Or, when you show up at the doorstep, they are going to say yes, come in.[11]

Shebala cites organizations like the NAJA and how it stresses diversity within the newsrooms. Shebala noted that mainstream journalists also need to "diversify" their minds.

> There is no excuse for them to not come out here and cover the reservation. . . . I don't care what color they are, and if they can't do that they aren't good journalists.

How many of us, we aren't mentally or physically challenged, but we cover those events. We cover men, women, we cover everything. I have my radio on. I read news. I'm watching news. . . . I go online. You just have to keep on top of it, if you are going to be any type of journalist.[12]

While Shebala believes mainstream news organizations should add Native communities as a beat, Chase Iron Eyes provided access to a digital Indigenous beat online. On Last Real Indians, Iron Eyes attempts to break down barriers by providing an online platform for all Indigenous voices. Iron Eyes believes that the younger Native generation's connection to the grid gives all media access to a variety of Native sources.

People in our generation—in their thirties, in their twenties—it is our turn right now for the next twenty years. We are the generation that has the good and bad connected to the grid, as it is changing the media worldwide.[13]

KBC utilizes social media to find a variety of Native people to interview for its programs. The network said oftentimes it is faster to get sources through social media than by phone or contacting people by e-mail.

Everyone has a Facebook, a Twitter account. . . . I know Natives in Florida. I know Natives in Alaska, Maine, and South Dakota. I know all these people. I can see their name on a Facebook page, get their information, and call them up instantly. I find out a little bit deeper about what is going on. Maybe it is something we can put out.[14]

Concurring with KBC, this study found that it was much easier to get in contact with Native journalists through Facebook compared to phone or e-mail.

Comparable to mainstream media, executive editor Bryan Pollard said the *Cherokee Phoenix* Facebook page is a digital conversation through which a diverse group of users can be visible and give their opinion. On the paper's social media page, he said, people share, comment, and like stories. What is unique to Native media is access to the views of a tight-knit community through social media. Pollard said the digital conversation creates an ongoing community dialogue surfacing from the more traditional medium of newspaper.[15]

Diverse media are turning to these nontraditional platforms to have the "digital conversation" Pollard mentions.[16] People of color are now able to express their diverse views online from websites to blogs. Platforms like YouTube allow for an alternative to information about different cultures. For example, one of the most watched series of videos in 2011 was posted by a younger group of Asian Americans. The videos showed Asian Americans in roles that traditional media do not show—a range of Asian Americans as musicians, artists, and dancers.[17]

The lack of Native journalists in mainstream newsrooms creates a lack of knowledge and access to Native people. The inadequate understanding by non-Native communities keeps misconceptions of the American Indian community alive. Stereotypes and the historical mistreatment of American Indians created a divide between those outside and inside Native communities. To break the barriers between mainstream and Native media, journalists need to visit and connect with Native communities, understanding the richness of Indian Country's diversity.

Cultivating Native Media Leaders at a Young Age

This book's fifth research question sought to understand the future of Native news and how current Native journalists became involved. Perhaps an answer to the future of Native media can be found by examining the road traveled by current Native journalists. Journalists understand stories through a personal filter. This filter is especially important to understand with Native people, who as a community have endured endless discrimination.

This study investigated why leading Native journalists became interested in the profession. Most journalists said it was when they were young that a mentor recommended they enter the field. Native journalists noted that they typically enjoyed reading, writing, and telling stories in the Native tradition, and this naturally connected them to the journalism profession.

Indian Country considers past NAJA president Paul DeMain a leader in journalism and advancing digital information. His path to journalism began as a junior at Wausau West High School in Wisconsin and an assignment by an inspirational English teacher who encouraged DeMain's poetic style of writing. "One of my English teachers liked how much I wrote. I never have been good at English punctuation, and I still struggle with it, but I was a prolific writer."[18]

DeMain ran away from home at the age of sixteen, but his English teacher had him record his writings in a journal. He missed a semester of school, but he gave his teacher the diary and the teacher passed him for the class. "He [the teacher] thought for Native people it would be better for people to be able to write their own stories rather than be held captive by non-Natives writing about us."[19]

The woman known as the "First Lady of Native Radio," Peggy Berryhill, also became interested in telling stories at a young age. "I can literally remember writing articles in the third grade and reading them and having the attention of the classroom. When I was in high school, I was on the high school newspaper."[20] While she said she didn't feel confident enough to go to college for writing, she has made huge strides in Native media. This award-winning producer founded the Native Media Resource Center, which is a media organization that promotes racial and cross-cultural harmony by producing content about Indigenous communities. The organization works with key Native media networks such as Native American Public Telecommunications, Inc., and the National Museum of the American Indian.[21]

In January 2012, this "First Lady of Native Radio" launched the only Native station in California that provides multilingual programming to the Pomo and Latino communities.[22] At this time, Berryhill was the only employee at KGUA. Berryhill worked sixty hours a week to get the station up and running. She started out at a bilingual Indigenous newspaper in Deacon, California. The paper was the only international press reporting on Natives in Central and South America. In 1973, Berryhill made the switch to radio and hosted a show called *Indian Time* for five years at public radio station KPFA in Berkeley, California. She said she missed connecting with people in the community, and that is why she got back into journalism.

Similar to Berryhill, Patty Talahongva, former president of the NAJA and current independent multimedia producer, became interested in journalism as a young woman. She said she read all the time and wrote to pen pals and to her uncle in the military. She said it was her high school counselor who recognized her writing talent.

> When I got into a high school, I was very fortunate. I went to a government boarding school in Phoenix . . . the local paper at the time had a newspaper insert on Saturdays for students. The stories were written by correspondents from all the different high schools in the Phoenix Metro valley. They never had a reporter from the Phoenix Indian High School. My high school counselor said you like to write . . . you aren't afraid to talk to people. She got me in touch with the editors at the paper, and they were thrilled. They never had correspondents from the boarding school.[23]

Talahongva worked for the highest rated CBS affiliate in Phoenix and learned skills from reporting to managing an assignment desk. "It grew from there. Hey, this is something I can do for a living, I can actually be in front of the news, write it, report it, and my career took off."[24]

A need for news and information on reservations led more than one Native journalist to start a communication organization, and this included DeMain. He started Indian Country Communications after working as a political appointee for the Wisconsin's governor's office. He had previously been employed with his tribe on the newspaper but was appointed to the state cabinet to represent American Indian issues. In 1986, after four years in politics, DeMain returned to the reservation and noticed that while he was gone the newspaper had gone defunct. He and a small group of people decided to start Indian Country Communications with the goal of becoming a Native News hub.[25] Within four to five years, the paper went national and ended up providing news to one hundred cities across the United States and Canada. At the height of Indian Country's subscriptions, *News from Indian Country* received approximately ten thousand subscribers from seventeen foreign countries.

Now, Indian Country Communications is a multifaceted business streaming events live online and through its mobile application, providing daily video news stories, continually updating its website and social media, publishing its newspaper, and owning key media property on the reservation such as the trading post. The company has produced more than 2,500 digital video programs for Indian Country from fourteen seconds to seven hours in length.[26]

Similar to DeMain noticing the lack of Native news on his reservation, the current station manager for the only Native owned-and-operated radio station in California, Joseph Orozco, returned to his home to start his first journalism job by launching and becoming the editor of a Native newspaper.[27] Orozco had not lived on the Hoopa Valley reservation in thirty years. He noticed there was not a Native newspaper in his area, and he received funding from a local church to launch the paper.

Later, Orozco decided to go into radio and is now the station manager for his tribal radio station. He said KIDE is mostly a public affairs station, sharing news and health information on what the tribal council and its departments are doing. "They are not looking for investigative journalism, so we are going to leave that for someone else."[28]

In contrast, Marley Shebala is an award-winning investigative community journalist. She found her passion for journalism after seeking refuge from racism in a library as a child and reading the adventures of Sherlock Holmes.

I looked back at my childhood, and I spent a lot of time at the library. Not because I wanted to be in the library, but because I grew up in northern Utah. Brigham City, Utah. A small, small town, but they had a huge Indian boarding school there. . . . Kids can be very mean. They were very mean. Racism is learned and they were taught well. I remember being called a dirty Indian, a smelly Indian. All kind of names. So I didn't have that many friends, and so I went to the library.[29]

Shebala has witnessed great change in the journalism profession since she went to college in the 1970s at the University of New Mexico—the university surrounded by protests for American Indian, Latino, and women's rights. While she didn't graduate from college, she started out as a nursing student. Her mother was a registered nurse, and so she said she wanted to be a nurse; however, after seeing how some doctors treated the female nurses she decided she didn't want to be in that profession.

I was busy with my camera. I was running around doing stories. And then people started asking me when I was going to be graduating from journalism school. And I kept telling them I was in nursing. And then I realized I was really enjoying what I was doing so I switched my major.[30]

Shebala was involved in the University of New Mexico's Kiva Club, a Native word that describes an underground area for spiritual ceremonies. She was elected to the club's council and asked to confront the student newspaper about why they weren't covering Native student events, which led to the Kiva Club starting its own newspaper called the *Four Directions*.

They asked, well how many Native American students on campus? Well, what does that have to do with it? Well, there aren't that many of you. . . . It was really racist, you know? So I, of course, I argued with them. And then thought that this is a lost cause. There is just no way you are going to change that attitude so I went back, made my report, and told them this is going to be a waste of our energy and time. There's not many of us. There's a lot of stuff happening fast, and even if we made them do it, who knows if they'd do a good job. Then we'd have to be questioning their stories. Let's just start our own newspaper.[31]

Being a student and in journalism was not easy for Shebala. Not because of the educational work, but because of how this Navajo woman, who has won prestigious awards for investigative and community reporting from both national and state journalism organizations, battled racism in her classes and never graduated.

> I didn't finish. I was spending way too much time arguing with my professors. I had taken some pictures of some Navajo kids at this National Indian Association conference that was in Albuquerque, and they are wearing their traditional outfits. I turned them in, and my professor says, who are these kids in these strange garb? He would just make remarks like that, and then finally he pulled me aside and said, you know you need to stop taking pictures of your people and broaden your horizons. I said, you know, I will if you pull over your white students and tell them to stop taking picture of white people and broaden their horizons. And he was totally shocked.[32]

Native journalists endured racism and personal doubt within a society that traditionally has not been supportive of the Native world. Leading Native journalists in print and radio are becoming the leading Native journalists across digital platforms. These now digital journalists bring a wealth of experience, understanding of community, and triumph over adversity.

Longevity in Newsroom Equals History

This book's sixth research question examined how Native journalists recommend young American Indians learn to be effective professional storytellers as digital platforms continue to change. Native reporters are needed not only within mainstream but within Native media. Native news organizations said they need young journalists to move through the newsroom ranks; the development of young journalists would provide Native organizations with people who have a foundation built on a history of covering Native news. Currently, Native outlets and journalist organizations are advocating for youth in newsrooms and using digital media as tools for this recruitment.

Native journalists are frustrated with training youth who abandon the field. The *Navajo Times* said it is hard to replace a Navajo reporter, and it is important to have longevity in the newsroom. Jeanie Greene of *Heartbeat Alaska* said she personally trained more than twenty editors, and they are now working elsewhere.[33]

Navajo Times senior reporter Marley Shebala has trained a lot of young reporters during her twenty-two years at the newspaper. She said because of longevity in her Native newsroom she is able to obtain information faster than her younger counterparts.

> I have a lot of that history and so I end up mentoring, and you heard Noel, she'll ask me questions. Or, you know she is having trouble getting a resolution or something. I'll just text a council delegate that I know and that knows me, trusts me, probably not completely, but enough to give me a document.[34]

Native journalists stressed understanding *history* in covering stories is an essential act for budding young Native journalists. This history includes not only their tribe, but the tribe's connection to the federal government.

> Like this water settlement, it involves the treaties. In 1868 and before and after that. They are always referring to that. With states the water settlements used to be in federal court and then Congress decided that they were going to give that to state courts, but there is this history of rivalries. Really, it is one of the states has been very jealous of the tribe's relationship with the federal government because they see oh, the reservation is on state land so they should be state citizens and therefore apply to state laws, but the tribes say it is the other way around.[35]

Papers like the *Navajo Times* and *Cherokee Phoenix* advocate recruiting young people into journalism. The *Cherokee Phoenix* has a financial fellowship to support young people to come and work for the paper.[36] The *Navajo Times* recruits young people on the reservation to become interns. The paper said it feels this is especially important on the reservation because many schools have had budget cuts and no longer have school newspapers. The paper also said multimedia allow for more creativity and opportunities for jobs.

> We've always tried to promote journalism as a career that they could look into, and now that you got technology, new media, the area is wide open. You aren't just writing and editing or just being a photographer, you do everything nowadays. You are doing video, audio, and you are also doing print so the field is so wide open and that's what we do.[37]

At the time of this research, the *Navajo Times* had three Navajo interns. Within a week, they had hired an additional intern. The paper said it has had success with training students, essentially growing its own future Navajo reporters. The paper has employed journalists who have become professors or mainstream reporters or those who have started major online Native news networks. "We have seen certain individuals that have started with us real, real young. . . . We've seen some really good young people come through here. We have seen them expand with the talents they have been given."[38]

The Native community collectively understands that all things in life are full circle, including in journalism. To extend the Native voice, advocacy must continue within the Native press and communities to recruit future Native journalists. Opportunities through digital media provide a fruitful platform for young journalists to tell their stories. Native stories online are needed, as they provide authentic stories that combat uneducated stereotypical reporting.

CHAPTER 5

Digital Visibility

This book examined how emerging digital media are critical platforms providing diverse visibility for Indian Country. Non-Native citizens tend to visit sites aligning with their ideologies,[1] while online Native storytelling encourages cultural exposure for those who are vested in debunking stereotypical images. Storytelling is an important cultural component of American Indian life that defines and shapes Native communities.[2] Continuing, expanding, and authenticating Native journalism through digital media builds the rich tradition of storytelling.

Digital media are helping Native cultures take control and increase the visibility of their own narrative. Native people are producing their own stories connected to Native issues and distributed across digital platforms, permitting more exposure to American Indian communities by non-Native people.

The community quality of Facebook aids the digital movement with its ability to build conversation through one online post after another and appears to be popular with Native organizations and individuals. Native journalists use Twitter, but mostly to promote blogs and other forms of media that exceed its 140-character limit.

These digital platforms provide opportunities for Native people to craft and aggregate their own stories. The availability of these authentic stories increases American Indian visibility online and therefore possibly in mainstream media.

Digital media allow for the expansion of the American Indian community that can counteract the decades, if not centuries, of stereotypical portrayals.

Because of this opportunity, Native communities across the country have acknowledged the importance of digital platforms. Digitally connected tribes have assisted other Native areas with connectivity, illustrating how the American Indian community acknowledges the importance of digital media and the spreading of the Native voice. In doing this, digital media amplify Native voices, fortify their place in American society, and help guide them out of the trenches of invisibility.

Detail, Language, and Privacy in Storytelling and Culture

The ritual of storytelling can be compared to the ritual of journalism norms and routines because they include emphasis on rich language and detail. When a reader picks up a newspaper from a Native press, such as the typical thirty-four-page *Navajo Times*, the content is thick with community and culturally based stories. The paper doesn't contain, as many mainstream papers do, mostly national stories and syndicated columns. Instead, Native papers contain detailed, local stories with descriptive language that attempt to mirror the Native tongue and are rich in detail, context, and connotation.

While Native papers are saturated with news that affects the community, a different norm and routine—that of privacy—is directly connected to the Native culture, its civic role, and sourcing. In these hefty Native papers, a reader will not find stories that are too personal or uncomfortably private; instead, such matters are typically handled through tribal ceremonies, an opportunity for everyone involved to discuss and heal. If a matter affects the entire community, the Native press will discuss it, but discretely and in a way tying it to the collective audience rather than the individuals closely involved in the story. For example, family interviews about the death of a loved one will not take place until much later when the family has had time to grieve, and only then with family permission. This kind of restraint is almost nonexistent in the mainstream press where the names of domestic violence victims are frequently reported, television reporters knock on the doors of the family of homicide victims, and journalists cold-call parents who have just tragically lost a child. These reporting methods often leave the victim feeling violated, marginalized, or even traumatized. The American Indian community's beliefs typically do not allow this type of reporting. Individuals and their beliefs are tied to the collective; if one suffers, the community suffers and beliefs are violated whether laws are broken or not. Because of this, Native news appears to be more thematic, rather than episodic, and more focused on solutions rather than consequences.

What perhaps makes the Native press very much unlike mainstream media is its definition of profitability. The lack of concern over what the mainstream defines as profit is tied to cultural beliefs; money is not the answer to helping a community thrive. Instead, sacredness to all living things is where most Native people truly find "profit," success, and fulfillment. The cancellation of the "Healing of the Earth Gathering" is an example of this. The medicine people planned to pray and give the respect deserved to the sacred San Francisco Peaks. Instead, conflict surrounded the mountains as the city of Flagstaff, along with the county and the state of Arizona, was working to use wastewater to create snow on these mountains for skiing. The *Navajo Times* believed this effort derailed the annual healing ceremony. Tom Arviso, CEO and publisher of the *Navajo Times*, said all the tribes—Navajos, Apaches, Pueblos, Zuni, and Hopi—united to voice opposition to these lifts. "What they are doing is really bad. In the Native eyes, it is one of the worst things you can do. It is like going and peeing on someone's lawn or defecating on a church lawn. Then laughing about it and leaving. No respect."[3] Arviso said when money, fame, and fortune are your priorities, your community will pay the price—supporting Native beliefs that all things are connected and everything happens for a reason. Even the Arizona drought in 2012 was considered a price paid for previous community actions.

Breaking through Stereotypical Coverage

Challenges exist for Native and mainstream digital media; both media groups are trying to decipher how to reach their audiences through emerging platforms such as mobile devices. However, Native media also have to battle preexisting, ingrained narratives comprised of stereotypes or perhaps, just as bad, the lack of a Native perspective at all. The main challenge is to circulate Native voices. But this movement is exacerbated by lack of infrastructure, diverging populations, and existing, untrue beliefs about Native communities.

More than 550 American Indian tribes exist in the United States,[4] and each American Indian tribe contains unique stories. Despite this diversity, some similarities in these stories do span Native communities, ranging from community event stories to environmental stories to sports stories.[5] Providing a diverse view digitally not only affects who gets news and who is heard, but also how the world views the United States.[6]

While conducting interviews at the *Navajo Times*, Victoria observed that sports were comparable to community gathering. The press operator Leonard Sylvan, who worked at the paper for more than twenty years, said he didn't attend all the sports but felt connected to the games by seeing all the Navajos in the pictures in the paper. Head photographer Paul Natonabah said his busiest time of the year was covering all the sports tournaments. Sports, specifically basketball, are a staple in many Native communities. The shoe company Nike has even noticed this passion. Nike has its own line of tennis shoes for American Indians, promoted by Native athletes.[7]

A recent story that most Native media outlets, as well as some mainstream, covered was the remarkable story of the Schimmel sisters. Shoni and Jude Schimmel, enrolled members of the Umatilla tribe with Paiute and Nez Perce ancestry, are two Native college basketball players who helped lead the University of Louisville basketball team to the Women's Final Four tournament.[8] While outsiders may not understand why the *Navajo Times*, for instance, led with this story on its main page, even non-Navajos who have some education about the passion of the Navajo Nation would understand why the story of these sisters is so salient.

"Rez ball," or reservation basketball, is a passion for many in the Navajo Nation. One social media site defined this style of basketball as "a ferocious, attacking style of basketball, fueled by passion, creativity, and relentless aggressiveness."[9] As Indian Country Today Media Network (ICTMN) wrote, "on many reservations across the country, Jude and Shoni Schimmel are shining a new light on a favorite sport, illuminating dreams born on dirt courts with bent, rusted rims."[10] ICTMN explains that while these two sisters prepared for the NCAA tournament, twenty high schools on the Navajo Nation were playing in the Arizona and New Mexico championships. The high school gyms for these teams are as large as some on college campuses. Much like in Kentucky, where schools are given a day off for the Kentucky Derby, or in Louisiana, where schools and businesses are given time off for Mardi Gras, the American Indian community celebrated basketball by taking time off to watch the Schimmel sisters play.

Many Native fans drove across the country to watch the sisters play in the Final Four, even if they had no ties to the University of Louisville, and those who couldn't make the trip constructed their support on social media. Athlete fan pages emerged on Facebook noting that Shoni was a role model: "SO PROUD OF Shoni and Jude. Native American Role Models for our youth. You two made my Heart swell with Pride. Now My Sonny Boys know that they can also play college ball. And they can accomplish what dreams they have . . . NATIVEPRIDE."[11] The *Navajo Times* conducted a phone interview with the two sisters from Oregon and said they might help challenge stereotypes much like professional basketball player Jeremy Lin did with the Asian American community.

The story of the Schimmel sisters attracted attention to Rez ball and directed American society's eclectic eye toward a different image of American Indians. Emerging media helped propel the story, and one Native news organization expressed excitement about the salience of Rez ball and how it made headlines the day before the championship game.[12]

The *Navajo Times* called it the "Schimmel shake," two college basketball players who are American Indian and made it to the Final Four.[13] In a sense, the story became a female version of Boston Red Sox outfielder Jacoby Ellsbury and followed in the footsteps of legendary Native American athlete Jim Thorpe, an Olympic gold medalist and football player in the early 1900s.[14]

On Monday, the eve of Louisville's national title showdown with Connecticut, Shoni Schimmel noted that her mother reared her and her siblings telling stories about Thorpe.

> One thing that my mom has talked to me about is, you have to go out there and show that you can come off a reservation and you can make it. Not a lot of people believe in Native Americans because they just get so comfortable with living on the reservation, because it is very comfortable. We love it there. It's always nice to be there. But at the same time, you have to get out of your comfort zone.[15]

This example illustrates Native news stories are covered by mainstream media if the topics are extreme success stories (sports superstar or famous actor) or conflicts. But it also shows how mainstream media can break through the stereotypes to celebrate the heritage of two young Native women who play basketball. The sisters' authentic voices and story can help change views. Unfortunately, these stories are few and far between in the mainstream media. Native news outlets must change the tide by staying committed to their community, their heritage, and the craft of digital journalism.

Native Norms and Routines and Digital Media-Crafting of Content and Distribution

Digital media are changing Native norms and routines, influencing how these news organizations craft and distribute content. New media provide access to Indigenous people across the world. Native news organizations use Facebook to find news stories and sources for these stories. For example, if a journalist was interested in writing or producing a story about someone traveling in their community to see the Schimmel sisters play in the Final Four in New Orleans, Facebook may be a resource Native news organizations can use to find sources within their tight-knit community.

Providing access to Natives across the world may alter the word "community" to include those participating online as well, therefore broadening the community's scope. American Indians, such as in the case with the *Cherokee Phoenix*, engage in digital conversations spawned by traditional news media. Native newspapers noted that readers extend the conversation of their coverage by discussing stories read in traditional media outlets through social media. The *Cherokee Phoenix* and *Navajo Times* find that users often seek out their websites or Facebook pages to keep a discussion alive online, after readers consume the more traditional form of the news such as a newspaper. Different angles on stories evolve as discussion continues on the Internet, providing additional authentic Native perspectives and voices.

Thanks to this broadened sense of community, the digital divide appears to be shrinking in Indian Country. Younger American Indians want news faster, and while the traditional forms of Native media, word of mouth, newspaper, and radio, still serve an older less digitally connected sector of the community, younger Natives are accustomed to accessing information through devices such as mobile phones. These younger groups appear to want a quicker turnaround on Native news. A growing digital audience is extending the authentic Native voice, while serving the niche audiences within the Native community.

Mobile connectivity provides an opportunity for American Indian communities both to experience the language and to help bridge the digital divide beyond the newsroom. For example, Native American Public Telecommunications, Inc. (NAPT) launched a smartphone application through which users can hear four different Native languages while seeing pictures of fourteen animals.[16] The NAPT application is just one of many applications online where users can learn and even write Native languages. Some Native applications even help teach young children how to speak traditional Native languages. In 2010, the Cherokee Nation worked with Apple, and the written form of the Cherokee language appears now on iPhones and iPads and is available through the Cherokee Nation's website as an added font.[17] Looking ahead, connectivity creates an opportunity for news consumers to view community events live from reservations. Paul DeMain's Indian Country TV provided live streaming for Memorial Day from Kinnamon School Veterans Memorial site on the Lac Courte Oreilles Ojibwe Reservation.[18]

Stereotypes of a Forgotten Community

American Indians are not consistently visible within mainstream media or their audiences. This invisibility leads to a marginalized group becoming more detached and a dominant society relying on unrealistic information and images. Native journalists felt that a main reason stereotypical coverage occurs is because the history of American Indians is painful, a history of oppression, slavery, death, and other mistreatment. An acknowledgement of these communities must involve an educated acknowledgement of the past, including from people who reflect and embody the Native's point of view. The American Indians observed and interviewed for this research viewed the Internet as a vehicle for offering counter-stereotypes and providing more truthful information and images.

Despite its painful past, the Native community typically doesn't view itself as victimized. In contrast, "plight" (an unfortunate situation) was a word one main-stream national news organization constantly repeated in recent coverage of an American Indian community, instead of referring to the history (longitudinal, not isolated) and progress of the community. At the same time that American Indians are not victims, they also do not fall into starkly polemic categories, such as noble savages or barbarian warriors. American Indians are nurses, teachers, professional sports athletes, lawyers, writers, journalists, rodeo stars, bodybuilders, bloggers, and the list goes on and on; however, mainstream media only report on American Indian communities, if they report at all, during specific circumstances. Having a story running consistently on Thanksgiving from one Native's point of view does not equal full coverage of a community.

Similarly, covering American Indian communities only when dramatic conflict exists is also not the answer—true of coverage for any community. If one turns on the news at any given moment, lead stories are usually disaster, crime, and other conflicts, and the newscast may occasionally ends with a heartwarming story. An array of communal stories can be told from multiple angles. However, the mainstream media often craft a perpetual, single narrative of minority groups that often includes chasing drama and covering conflict-driven stories that demonstrate to readers and viewers that these are the most important narratives. Context, depth, and resolution are reported rarely—and even less when the story is about Indian Country. However, lack of rich reporting is not a problem only with Native coverage, but with coverage overall. The effects are heightened when applied to Native coverage. Stereotypes provide no solution to tragic events and instead perpetuate the idea that Natives are victims—which the journalists indicate goes beyond stereotyping and impacts who they are as a community and a people.

To truly understand and report on a community, a journalist must be immersed in the community's history and context. A shortfall of mainstream media and of most non-Natives is that they have not visited these reservations to note media usage themselves, yet some still attempt to report on Indian Country. These non-Natives do not understand the strong bond and connection within this community, and more importantly they don't understand lifestyles on the reservation. If mainstream journalists considered this community as a news beat, it would allow for mainstream media to provide more representative, nonstereotypical coverage of this community.

Fortunately, there is a desire to increase American Indian visibility in professional and academic arenas. For non-Native organizations, attempts should be made to recruit from within Native communities. For example, instead of just advertising or promoting jobs and educational opportunities through mainstream routes, visit reservations and contact Native organizations to promote opportunities.

Connect and Grow Native Journalists as an Answer to Stereotypes

American Indian research tends to focus on well-documented and well-analyzed stereotypes, an issue that has existed since Europeans first began colonization. This study hopes to move the academic and professional discussions beyond exhausted stereotypes and more toward solutions offered by emerging media. One solution offered by online Native media is an understanding that culture is not synonymous with costumes—a mainstream practice that historically has lent itself to positioning American Indians as "other" and unimportant.

Coverage of any community should include many angles and inclusive opinions within that area, and thanks to social media, these perspectives are now readily available online. The mainstream media should be especially reflective of groups who are marginalized within society, not just covering these groups when there is a crisis or negative story but instead seeing the community more as a beat—checking on and visiting it frequently.[19]

Conclusion

A main finding within this research helping build theory within American Indian media research is American Indian media have a strong connection to culture and community through their storytelling. The Native connection to community and culture is extending online through digital platforms, and much like Native language, Native stories covered in this medium are reported with thick, rich cultural detail. Reporters who worked for both the Native and the mainstream press noted they could not write in this more detailed fashion when they covered stories for their non-Native newsrooms.

Unlike mainstream media, stories considered private are discussed in a ceremonial setting, and out of respect, the Native press typically avoids covering them in detail. This respect does not mean stories are not reported if they affect the entire community; however, unlike mainstream media, the press does not try to bombard families, for example, in the case of death. Instead, reporters make contact with the family and attempt to speak with its members openly at a more appropriate time.

Because Native media have different reporting methods, a digital divide still exists within Indian Country; however, the presence and usage of mobile technology by American Indians and Native news is shrinking this gap.[20] Native youth have a desire for Native news in a more timely fashion than the tradition weekly tribal publications offer.[21] American Indian news consumers are having digital conversations online—spreading Native news found in traditional media and advancing these news stories with circulation and online discussions in social media arenas such as Facebook and Twitter.[22]

Digital media are changing Native news organizations. American Indian media are using the Internet to distribute programming and to search for sources as well as story ideas. The digital form of media allows anyone who has the desire to seek out and connect with American Indian perspectives. This broadens the scope of Native storytelling, connecting the tight-knit community even further while at the same time raising visibility to non-Natives.

The American Indian population is expected to grow exponentially in the next forty years, and as our society becomes more diverse it is essential to value, respect, and educate oneself about different cultures.[23] American Indian journalists suggest the answer to combating the stereotypical views is for non-Natives to connect with American Indians, whether online or on a reservation or both. This connection allows for others to understand more about the American Indian culture and to be more aware of the stereotypes that are accepted within our daily society.

One method of defying these stereotypes is to support and recruit additional American Indians who are familiar with Native storytelling to enter the field of journalism. This effort has existed for some time. Some progress has been made (not as much as had been hoped), so this effort should go even further: American Indian media owners, and having American Indians elevated to top management positions. American Indian media advocate increasing the number of American Indians entering journalism. As Native journalists noted, longevity is essential within the Native media profession. Many issues covered within the Native press have a long-standing history, and so incoming journalists must understand the history of the culture, community, and perspective.

When American Indian news organizations lose a single Native journalist, they lose much more than just an employee because of that person's understanding of Indian history and culture. Native journalists interviewed in this study said they actively reach out to youth in their communities because they understand the importance of cultivating future Native journalists who will serve as the voices of the next generation.

This book provided a detailed picture, to our knowledge the most detailed, into how Native journalism is changing with digital media. We found that while American Indians are, like many other media professionals, using digital media to show their stories and connect with their audiences on an unprecedented scale, their storytelling culture is still the driving force of the content. Their stories are not controlled by the technology. The ritual of storytelling did not change a great deal in the Native community. The distribution and the eyes reached expanded on an incredible scale, and it may be a few generations before we are able to see what impact that has on those communities. In five or ten years, perhaps the digital divide will continue to diminish as more content on mobile phones and better connectivity increase information transmission to both urban and reservation areas. And as the digital divide shrinks, so too will the cultural divide.

Interview Guide

- Where do you go to find news?
- What news do you listen to, read, watch, etc.?
- How did you find out about the news sources you access?
- How have you seen news changing in your community over the past couple years?
- Do you feel that emerging media is extending the ritual of storytelling within your community?
- Do you think there is a difference between the ways American Indian media cover stories compared to non-Native media?
- How do you think mainstream media could serve Native communities better?
- What do you feel are the most important community issues to cover?
- How do Native media cover these important social issues compared to non-Native media?
- What is missing in coverage?
- What do you think is the most important way emerging media can be used in the future within your community?

- As information transmission has changed with emerging media, do you feel American Indian media are growing online?
- How do resources affect your coverage of storytelling?
- What are the barriers to providing news through emerging media? Resources? Access? Cultural barriers?
- What resources do you find have the greatest impact on your coverage?
- Do you see mainstream media making strides to connect with Native communities?
- How do you feel you serve your community?
- How is covering the story for the radio, newspaper, or television different from covering a story online or through social media?
- Do you feel that emerging media adds or detracts from cultural information provided to news consumers?
- What cultural news is not appropriate for online? Where and how do you find the balance? Who decides? Individual, news organization, or tribe?
- What is the responsibility of a Native journalist in covering stories? How does this extend to emerging media? Do you find it is a collective decision or a societal responsibility of a journalist?

Demographics

- What community do you live in?
- How long have you lived there?
- What is your age?
- What is your gender?
- What tribe/s do you belong to?

Notes

Introduction

1. V. Merina, "The Internet: Continuing the Legacy of Storytelling," *Nieman Reports*, fall 2005, 32–34.

2. N. Shoemaker, *Clearing a Path: Theorizing the Past in Native American Studies* (New York: Psychology Press, 2002); B. Duncan, *Living Stories of the Cherokee* (Chapel Hill: University of North Carolina Press, 1998).

3. Duncan, *Living Stories of the Cherokee.*

4. J. Lule, *Daily News, Eternal Stories: The Mythological Role of Journalism* (New York: Guilford Press, 2001).

5. J. Meness, "Smoke Signals as Equipment for Living," in *American Indians and the Mass Media*, ed. M. G. Carstarphen and J. P. Sanchez (Norman: University of Oklahoma Press, 2012), 94–112; Shoemaker, *Clearing a Path*; E. Cook-Lynn, "American Indian Intellectualism and the New Indian Story," *American Indian Quarterly* 20, no. 1 (1996): 57–76.

6. C. C. Wilson, F. Gutiérrez, and L. M. Chao, *Racism, Sexism, and the Media: Multicultural Issues into the New Communications Age*, 4th ed. (Los Angeles: Sage, 2013).

7. J. A. Avila-Hernandez, "Native Americans in the Twenty-First Century Newsroom: Breaking through Barriers in New Media," in Carstarphen and Sanchez, *American Indians*

and the Mass Media, 227–31.

8. S. G. Phillips, "'Indians on Our Warpath': World War II Images of Native Americans in *Life* Magazine, 1937–1949," in Carstarphen and Sanchez, *American Indians and the Mass Media*, 50.

9. J. M. Krogstad, "Social Media Preferences Vary by Race and Ethnicity," Pew Research Center, February 3, 2015, http://www.pewresearch.org.

10. V. Sanchez, "Buying into Racism: American Indian Product Icons in the American Marketplace," in Carstarphen and Sanchez, *American Indians and the Mass Media*, 153–69.

11. Phillips, "'Indians on Our Warpath,'" 41.

12. Peggy Berryhill, president/general manager, KGUA, interview with authors, February 1, 2015.

13. V. Schilling, "The Revenant's Elk Dog: A Conversation with Duane Howard," Indian Country Today Media Network, February 4, 2016, http://indiancountrytodaymedianetwork.com.

14. S. Moya-Smith, "New Anti-Redskins Video Says FedEx 'Embraces Racism,'" Indian Country Today Media Network, September 4, 2014, http://indiancountrytodaymedianetwork.com.

15. Barry Wilner, "Simms, Dungy likely not to use 'Redskins' on TV," Associated Press, August 18, 2014.

16. Suzan Harjo, president and executive director, Morning Star Institute, interview with authors, February 12, 2015. See also ICTMN Staff, "Suzan Harjo to Receive Presidential Medal of Freedom," Indian Country Today Media Network, November 11, 2014, http://indiancountrytodaymedianetwork.com; "Suzan Shown Harjo," American Program Bureau, http://www.apbspeakers.com/speaker/suzan-shown-harjo.

17. Harjo, interview, February 12, 2015.

18. "What We Do," U.S. Department of the Interior, Indian Affairs, http://www.bia.gov/.

19. M. McDonnell-Smith, "Asians Are Fastest-Growing U.S. Ethnic Group, Blacks Are Slowest, Reports U.S. Census Bureau," Diversity Inc., June 17, 2013, http://www.diversityinc.com.

20. U.S. Census Bureau, "American Indians by the Numbers," Infoplease, 2012, http://www.infoplease.com.

21. "President Barack Obama Wins a Second Term in the White House," Indianz.com, November 7, 2012, http://www.indianz.com; J. Murphy, "Technology Specialists Help Advance Cherokee Language," *Cherokee Phoenix*, March 11, 2013, http://www.cherokeephoenix.org.

22. Rhonda LeValdo, president, Native American Journalists Association, interview with

authors, November 6, 2012.

23. *Navajo Times*, http://navajotimes.com.

24. E. Grinberg, "Native American Designers Fight Cultural Caricatures," CNN, November 30, 2012, http://www.cnn.com.

25. C. Petill, "'Victoria's Secret Fashion Show' Leads CBS for the Night," *Examiner*, December 6, 2012, http://www.examiner.com.

26. M. N. Trahant, *Pictures of Our Nobler Selves* (Nashville: Freedom Forum First Amendment Center, 1995).

27. R. Entman and A. Rojecki, *The Black Image in the White Mind: Media and Race in America* (Chicago: University of Chicago Press, 2001).

28. Trahant, *Pictures of Our Nobler Selves*.

29. Jeff Harjo, executive director, Native American Journalists Association, interview with authors, March 16, 2012; Bryan Pollard, executive editor, *Cherokee Phoenix*, interview with authors, February 14, 2012; Trahant, *Pictures of Our Nobler Selves*.

30. R. Chavez, "Joining the Circle: A Yakima Story," in Carstarphen and Sanchez, *American Indians and the Mass Media*, 232–34; Pollard, interview, February 14, 2012; Marley Shebala, senior reporter, *Navajo Times*, interview with authors, June 2012.

31. J. Dunaway, "Markets, Ownership, and the Quality of Campaign News Coverage," *Journal of Politics* 70, no. 4 (2008): 1193–202.

32. K. R. Kemper, "Who Speaks for Indigenous Peoples? Tribal Journalists, Rhetorical Sovereignty, and Freedom of Expression," *Journalism & Communication Monographs* 12, no. 1 (2010): 3–58; C. G. Anderson, "American Indian Tribal Web Sites: A Review and Comparison," *Electronic Library* 21, no. 5 (2003): 450–55.

33. P. J. Shoemaker, and S. D. Reese, *Mediating the Message: Theories of Influences on Mass Media Content*, 2nd ed. (White Plains, NY: Longman, 1996).

34. Tom Arviso, executive officer and publisher, *Navajo Times*, interview with authors, July 19, 2012.

35. Marley Shebala, senior reporter, *Navajo Times*, interview with authors, July 20, 2012.

36. Arviso, interview, July 19, 2012.

37. Chase Iron Eyes, creator, Last Real Indians, interview with authors, January 13, 2012.

38. Pollard, interview, February 14, 2012.

39. J. Allen, "Ethnic Media Reaching Record Numbers in U.S.," CommonDreams. June 6, 2009, http://www.commondreams.org.

40. E. Guskin and A. Mitchell, "Innovating News in Native Communities," *The State of the News Media 2012*, Pew Research Center Project for Excellence in Journalism, http://stateofthemedia.org; Allen, "Ethnic Media Reaching Record Numbers."

41. Wilson, Gutierrez, and Chao, *Racism, Sexism, and the Media.*

42. R. S. Izard, *Diversity That Works* (Baton Rouge: Louisiana State University Press, 2008).

43. Allen, "Ethnic Media Reaching Record Numbers"; R. Srinivasan, "Indigenous, Ethnic and Cultural Articulations of New Media," *International Journal of Cultural Studies* 9, no. 4 (2006): 497–518.

44. Izard, *Diversity That Works.*

45. Pollard, interview, February 14, 2012.

46. *"Cherokee Phoenix,"* Online Books Page, http://onlinebooks.library.upenn.edu.

47. Pollard, interview, February 14, 2012.

48. Pollard, interview, February 14, 2012.

49. Guskin and Mitchell, "Innovating News in Native Communities."

50. Rebecca Landsberry, membership and communications manager, Native American Journalists Association, interview with authors, July 6, 2015.

51. Trahant, *Pictures of Our Nobler Selves.*

52. J. Harjo, interview, March 16, 2012.

53. K. Mossberger, C. J. Tolbert, and M. C. Stansbury, *Virtual Inequality: Beyond the Digital Divide* (Washington, DC: Georgetown University Press, 2003).

54. J. Harjo, interview, March 16, 2012; Noel Lyn Smith, reporter, *Navajo Times*, interview with authors, June 2012.

55. Roy Boney, "Cherokeespace.com: Native Social Networking," in Carstarphen and Sanchez, *American Indians and the Mass Media*, 222–26.

56. J. Harjo, interview, March 16, 2012.

57. Guskin and Mitchell, "Innovating News in Native Communities."

58. Guskin and Mitchell, "Innovating News in Native Communities."

59. J. Harjo, interview, March 16, 2012.

60. ICTMN Staff, "Broadband in Indian Country to Expand," Indian Country Today Media Network, March 3, 2011, http://indiancountrytodaymedianetwork.com.

Chapter 1. Native Storytelling

1. C. C. Wilson, F. Gutiérrez, and L. M. Chao, *Racism, Sexism, and the Media: Multicultural Issues into the New Communications Age*, 4th ed. (Los Angeles: Sage, 2013), 244.

2. Wilson, Gutiérrez, and Chao, *Racism, Sexism, and the Media.*

3. N. Shoemaker, *Clearing a Path: Theorizing the Past in Native American Studies* (New York: Psychology Press, 2002); B. Duncan, *Living Stories of the Cherokee* (Chapel Hill: University of North Carolina Press, 1998).

4. I. Piller, "Passing for a Native Speaker: Identity and Success in Second Language

Learning," *Journal of Sociolinguistics* 6, no. 2 (2002): 179.

5. J. Carey, "A Cultural Approach to Communication," in *Communication as Culture: Essays on Media and Society* (New York: Routledge, 1992), 18.

6. Carey, "A Cultural Approach to Communication."

7. J. B. Singer, "Strange Bedfellows? The Diffusion of Convergence in Four News Organizations," *Journalism Studies* 5, no. 1 (2004): 3–18.

8. H. Schwarz, "Colorado Theater Shooting Witnesses Take to Twitter and Reddit to Share Their Stories," Media-ite, July 20, 2012, http://www.mediaite.com; C. Warren, "Colorado Theater Shooting: How It Played out Online," Mashable, July 20, 2012, http://mashable.com.

9. Schwarz, "Colorado Theater Shooting Witnesses Take to Twitter and Reddit to Share Their Stories."

10. J. B. Singer, "The Metro Wide Web: Changes in Newspapers' Gatekeeping Role Online," *Journalism & Mass Communication Quarterly* 78, no. 1 (2001): 65–80.

11. D. Gross, "Twitter User Unknowingly Reported bin Laden Attack," CNN, May 2, 2011, http://www.cnn.com.

12. L. Grossman, "Iran Protests: Twitter, the Medium of the Movement," *TIME*, June 17, 2009, http://www.time.com.

13. T. Sakaki, M. Okazaki, and Y. Matsuo, "Earthquake Shakes Twitter Users: Real-time Event Detection by Social Sensors" (unpublished paper presented at the International World Wide Web Conference, Raleigh, NC, April 2010).

14. R. Boney, "Cherokeespace.com: Native Social Networking," in *American Indians and the Mass Media*, ed. M. G. Carstarphen and J. P. Sanchez (Norman: University of Oklahoma Press, 2012), 222–26.

15. G. L. Daniels, "The Role of Native American Print and Online Media in the 'Era of Big Stories': A Comparative Case Study of Native American Outlets' Coverage of the Red Lake Shootings," *Journalism* 7, no. 3 (2006): 321–42; L. Roy and D. Raitt, "The Impact of IT on Indigenous Peoples," *Electronic Library* 21, no. 5 (2003): 411–13.

16. L. Mitten, "Indians on the Internet—Selected Native American Web Sites," *Electronic Library* 21, no. 5 (2003): 443–49.

17. Native Voice One, http://www.nv1.org.

18. K. Mossberger C. J. Tolbert, and M. C. Stansbury, *Virtual Inequality: Beyond the Digital Divide* (Washington, DC: Georgetown University Press, 2003), 1.

19. E. Guskin and A. Mitchell, "Innovating News in Native Communities," *The State of the News Media 2012*, Pew Research Center Project for Excellence in Journalism, http://stateofthemedia.org.

20. Mossberger, Tolbert, and Stansbury, *Virtual Inequality*.

21. Monica Anderson, "Racial and Ethnic Differences in How People Use Mobile Technology," Pew Research Center, http://www.pewresearch.org.

22. Wilson, Gutiérrez, and Chao, *Racism, Sexism, and the Media*.

23. D. Berkowitz, *Cultural Meanings of News: A Text-Reader* (Los Angeles: Sage, 2010).

24. P. J. Shoemaker and S. D. Reese, *Mediating the Message: Theories of Influences on Mass Media Content*, 2nd ed. (White Plains, NY: Longman, 1996).

25. Wilson, Gutiérrez, and Chao, *Racism, Sexism, and the Media*; D. Berkowitz, *Social Meanings of News: A Text-Reader* (Los Angeles: Sage, 1997).

26. G. Tuchman, *Making News: A Study in the Construction of Reality* (New York: Free Press, 1978).

27. Wilson, Gutiérrez, and Chao, *Racism, Sexism, and the Media*.

28. S. Hall, "The Rediscovery of 'Ideology': Return of the Repressed in Media Studies," in *Culture, Society and the Media*, ed. M. Gurevitch, J. Curran, T. Bennett, and J. Wollacott (London: Methuen, 1982).

29. Wilson, Gutiérrez, and Chao, *Racism, Sexism, and the Media*; C. P. Campbell, *Race and News: Critical Perspectives* (New York: Routledge, 2012).

30. T. E. Cook, *Governing with the News* (Chicago, IL: University of Chicago Press, 1998).

31. N. Eliasoph, "Routines and the Making of Oppositional News," *Critical Studies in Mass Communication* 5 (1988): 313–34.

32. J. Dunaway, "Markets, Ownership, and the Quality of Campaign News Coverage," *Journal of Politics* 70, no. 4 (2008): 1193–202.

33. B. I. Page, "The Mass Media as Political Actors," *PS: Political Science and Politics* 29, no. 1 (1996): 20–24.

34. Wilson, Gutiérrez, and Chao, *Racism, Sexism, and the Media*.

35. T. E. Cook, "Afterword: Political Values and Production Values," *Political Communication* 13 (1996): 469–81; J. G. Blumler and M. Gurevitch, "Politicians and the Press: An Essay on Role Relationships," in *Handbook of Political Communication*, ed. D. D. Nimmo and K. R. Sanders (Beverly Hills: Sage, 1981), 467–93.

36. H. Molotch and M. Lester, "News as Purposive Behavior: On the Strategic Use of Routine Events, Accidents, and Scandals," *American Sociological Review* 30 (1974): 101–12.

37. D. D. Kurpius, "Sources and Civic Journalism: Changing Patterns of Reporting?," *Journalism & Mass Communication Quarterly* 79, no. 4 (2002): 853–66.

38. W. L. Bennett, "Toward a Theory of Press–State Relations in the United States," *Journal of Communication* 40, no. 2 (1990): 103–27.

39. Kurpius, "Sources and Civic Journalism."

40. C. M. Swain, *Black Faces, Black Interests: The Representation of African Americans in Congress* (Lanham, MD: University Press of America, 2006). L. J. Hanks, *The Struggle for Black Political Empowerment in Three Georgia Counties* (Knoxville: University of Tennessee Press, 1987).

41. Kurpius, "Sources and Civic Journalism."

42. P. M. Poindexter, L. Smith, and D. Heider, "Race and Ethnicity in Local Television News: Framing, Story Assignments, and Source Selections," *Journal of Broadcasting & Electronic Media* 47, no. 4 (2003): 524–36; S. Jha and R. S. Izard, "Who Got to Talk about It: Sourcing and Attribution in Broadcast News Coverage of the First 24 Hours of the 9/11 Tragedy," *Seattle Journal for Social Justice* 4, no. 1 (2005): 101–18.

43. Campbell, *Race and News.*

44. Jha and Izard, "Who Got to Talk about It."

45. A. Miller and V. Bemker LaPoe, "Sourcing in National vs. Local Television News Coverage of the Deepwater Horizon Oil Spill: A Study of Experts, Victims, Roles and Race" (paper presented at the Association for Education in Journalism and Mass Communication conference, St. Louis, MO, August 2011); A. Miller and S. Roberts, "Visual Agenda-Setting & Proximity after Hurricane Katrina: A Study of Those Closest to the Event," *Visual Communication Quarterly* 17, no. 1 (2010): 31–46.

46. E. N. Ben-Porath and L. K. Shaker, "News Images, Race, and Attribution in the Wake of Hurricane Katrina," *Journal of Communication* 60, no. 3 (2010): 466–90; Miller and Roberts, "Visual Agenda-Setting & Proximity after Hurricane Katrina"; S. Kahle, N. Yu, and E. Whiteside, "Another Disaster: An Examination of Portrayals of Race in Hurricane Katrina Coverage," *Visual Communications Quarterly* 14, no. 2 (2007): 75–89.

47. Miller and Roberts, "Visual Agenda-Setting & Proximity after Hurricane Katrina."

48. Wilson, Gutiérrez, and Chao, *Racism, Sexism, and the Media.*

49. K. Reeves, *Voting Hopes or Fears? White Voters, Black Candidates and Racial Politics in America* (Oxford: Oxford University Press, 1997).

50. Wilson, Gutiérrez, and Chao, *Racism, Sexism, and the Media*; Campbell, *Race and News.*

51. Kurpius, "Sources and Civic Journalism."

52. J. T. Hamilton, *All the News That's Fit to Sell: How the Market Transforms Information into News* (Princeton, NJ: Princeton University Press, 2004); Aufderheide, 2004; J. H. McManus, *Market-Driven Journalism: Let the Citizen Beware?* (Los Angeles: Sage, 1994).

53. S. Allan and B. Zelizer, "Rules of Engagement: Journalism and War," in *Reporting War: Journalism in Wartime*, ed. S. Allan and B. Zelizer (New York: Routledge, 2004), 3–21. P. Aufderheide, "Big Media and Little Media: The Journalistic Informal Sector during the Invasion of Iraq," in *Reporting War: Journalism in Wartime*, ed. S. Allan and B. Zelizer

(New York: Routledge, 2004) 333–46.

54. Hamilton, *All the News That's Fit to Sell.*

55. R. Seymour, "Names, not Nations: Patterned References to Indigenous Americans in the *New York Times* and *Los Angeles Times*, 1999–2000," in Carstarphen and Sanchez, *American Indians and the Mass Media*, 73–93.

56. Seymour, "Names, not Nations," 77.

57. Seymour, "Names, not Nations."

58. Wilson, Gutiérrez, and Chao, *Racism, Sexism, and the Media*; J. S. Ettema, "Crafting Cultural Resonance: Imaginative Power in Everyday Journalism," *Journalism* 6, no. 2 (2005): 131–52.

59. Ettema, "Crafting Cultural Resonance."

60. Wilson, Gutiérrez, and Chao, *Racism, Sexism, and the Media*; W. Lippmann, *Public Opinion* (New York: Harcourt, Brace, 1992); R. M. Entman, "Framing: Toward Clarification of a Fractured Paradigm," *Journal of Communication* 43, no. 4 (1993): 51–58.

61. Wilson, Gutiérrez, and Chao, *Racism, Sexism, and the Media*, 54.

62. Lippmann, *Public Opinion*; Entman, "Framing."

63. J. Lule, *Daily News, Eternal Stories: The Mythological Role of Journalism* (New York: Guilford Press, 2001); Berkowitz, *Cultural Meanings of News.*

64. Wilson, Gutiérrez, and Chao, *Racism, Sexism, and the Media.*

65. V. Sanchez, "Buying into Racism: American Indian Product Icons in the American Marketplace," in Carstarphen and Sanchez, *American Indians and the Mass Media*, 153–69.

66. I. Watson, "The Future Is Our Past: We Once Were Sovereign and We Still Are," *Indigenous Law Bulletin* 8, no. 3 (2012): 12–15; B. A. D. Keever, C. Martindale, and M. A. Weston, eds., *U.S. News Coverage of Racial Minorities: A Sourcebook, 1934–1996* (Westport, CT: Greenwood Press, 1997).

67. Watson, "The Future Is Our Past"; Keever, Martindale, and Weston, *U.S. News Coverage of Racial Minorities.*

68. D. Merskin, "Winnebagos, Cherokees, Apaches and Dakotas: The Persistence of Stereotyping of American Indians in American Advertising Brands," *Howard Journal of Communications* 12 (2001): 159–69; Wilson, Gutiérrez, and Chao, *Racism, Sexism, and the Media.*

69. Wilson, Gutiérrez, and Chao, *Racism, Sexism, and the Media.*

70. Wilson, Gutiérrez, and Chao, *Racism, Sexism, and the Media.*

71. M. E. Grabe and E. P. Bucy, *Image Bite Politics: News and the Visual Framing of Elections* (Oxford: Oxford University Press, 2009).

72. A. D. Pond Cummings, "A Shifting Wind? Media Stereotyping of American Indians and the Law," in Carstarphen and Sanchez, *American Indians and the Mass Media*, 185–212.
73. Wilson, Gutiérrez, and Chao, *Racism, Sexism, and the Media*.
74. L. Feldman, "The News about Comedy Young Audiences: *The Daily Show*, and Evolving Notions of Journalism," *Journalism* 8, no. 4 (2007): 406–27.
75. N. Postman, *Amusing Ourselves to Death: Public Discourse in the Age of Show Business* (New York: Penguin, 2006).
76. G. Gerbner, L. Gross, N. Signorielli, and M. Morgan, "Television Violence, Victimization, and Power," *American Behavioral Scientist* 23, no. 5 (1980): 705–16.
77. Wilson, Gutiérrez, and Chao, *Racism, Sexism, and the Media*, 84.
78. Wilson, Gutiérrez, and Chao, *Racism, Sexism, and the Media*, 76.
79. Wilson, Gutiérrez, and Chao, *Racism, Sexism, and the Media*, 74.
80. R. Entman and A. Rojecki, *The Black Image in the White Mind: Media and Race in America* (Chicago: University of Chicago Press, 2001).
81. Sanchez, "Buying into Racism"; Entman and Rojecki, *The Black Image in the White Mind*.
82. Entman and Rojecki, *The Black Image in the White Mind*.
83. J. Zaller, *The Nature and Origins of Mass Opinion* (Cambridge: Cambridge University Press, 1992).
84. S. T. Fiske, A. J. C. Cuddy, and P. Glick, "Universal Dimensions of Social Cognition: Warmth and Competence," *Trends in Cognitive Sciences* 11, no. 2 (2007): 77–83.
85. Wilson, Gutiérrez, and Chao, *Racism, Sexism, and the Media*; W. D. Sloan, *The Media in America: A History*, 8th ed. (Northrop, AL: Vision Press, 2011); Entman and Rojecki, *The Black Image in the White Mind*; J. L. Dates and W. Barlow, *Split Image: African Americans in the Mass Media*, 2nd ed. (Washington, DC: Howard University Press, 1993).
86. S. Hall, "The White of their Eyes: Racist Ideologies and the Media," in *Gender, Race, and Class in Media: A Text-Reader*, ed. G. Dines and J. M. Humez (Los Angeles: Sage, 1995).
87. T. Mendelberg, "A Theory of Racial Appeals," in *The Race Card: Campaign Strategy, Implicit Messages, and the Norm of Equality* (Princeton, NJ: Princeton University Press, 2001), 3–27.
88. Wilson, Gutiérrez, and Chao, *Racism, Sexism, and the Media*.
89. T. L. Dixon, "Crime News and Racialized Beliefs: Understanding the Relationship between Local News Viewing and Perceptions of African Americans and Crime," *Journal of Communication* 58, no. 1 (2008): 106–25; R. M. Entman, "Representation and Reality in the Portrayal of Black on Network Television News," *Journalism & Mass Communication Quarterly* 71, no. 3 (1994): 509–20; Gerbner et al., "Television Violence, Victimization, and Power."

90. T. L. Dixon and D. Linz, "Race and the Misrepresentation of Victimization on Local Television News," *Communication Research* 27, no. 5 (2000): 547–73.

91. Wilson, Gutiérrez, and Chao, *Racism, Sexism, and the Media.*

92. M. Kopacz and B. L. Lawton, "The YouTube Indian: Portrayals of Native Americans on a Viral Video Site," *New Media & Society* 13, no. 2 (2011): 330–49.

93. Sanchez, "Buying into Racism"; Merskin, "Winnebagos, Cherokees, Apaches and Dakotas."

94. Wilson, Gutiérrez, and Chao, *Racism, Sexism, and the Media*; Merskin, "Winnebagos, Cherokees, Apaches and Dakotas."

95. Wilson, Gutiérrez, and Chao, *Racism, Sexism, and the Media*, 40; S. G. Phillips, "'Indians on Our Warpath': World War II Images of Native Americans in *Life* Magazine, 1937–1949," in Carstarphen and Sanchez, *American Indians and the Mass Media*, 33–55.

96. Phillips, "'Indians on Our Warpath.'"

97. Kopacz and Lawton, "The YouTube Indian"; Merskin, "Winnebagos, Cherokees, Apaches and Dakotas."

98. Wilson, Gutiérrez, and Chao, *Racism, Sexism, and the Media.*

99. Wilson, Gutiérrez, and Chao, *Racism, Sexism, and the Media.*

100. L. D. Lieber, "Capitalizing on Demographic Change: How Your Organization Can Prepare for a Global Workplace," DiversityBusiness.com, http://www.diversitybusiness.com.

101. Wilson, Gutiérrez, and Chao, *Racism, Sexism, and the Media.*

102. Wilson, Gutiérrez, and Chao, *Racism, Sexism, and the Media*; Sanchez, "Buying into Racism."

103. D. McAuliffe Jr., "Elevating Journalism in Indian Country," American Society of Newspaper Editors, 2000, http://asne.org.

104. J. A. Avila-Hernandez, "Native Americans in the Twenty-First Century Newsroom: Breaking through Barriers in New Media," in Carstarphen and Sanchez, *American Indians and the Mass Media*, 227–31.

105. D. A. Mihesuah, *American Indians: Stereotypes and Realities* (Atlanta: Clarity, 1996); K. G. Swisher, "Why Indian People Should Be the Ones to Write about Indian Education," *American Indian Quarterly* 20, no. 1 (1996): 83–90.

106. J. Meness, "Smoke Signals as Equipment for Living," in Carstarphen and Sanchez, *American Indians and the Mass Media*, 94–112.

107. Watson, "The Future Is Our Past," 12; Keever, Martindale, and Weston, *U.S. News Coverage of Racial Minorities.*

108. Keever, Martindale, and Weston, *U.S. News Coverage of Racial Minorities.*

109. Watson, "The Future Is Our Past"; Keever, Martindale, and Weston, *U.S. News Coverage of Racial Minorities.*

110. Meness, "Smoke Signals as Equipment for Living," 96.

111. Meness, "Smoke Signals as Equipment for Living."

112. D. L. Fixico, "Ethics and Responsibilities in Writing American Indian History," *American Indian Quarterly* 20, no. 1 (1996): 29–39.

113. University of New Mexico, Human Research Protections Office, http://hsc.unm.edu/research/hrpo/.

114. Fixico, "Ethics and Responsibilities in Writing American Indian History."

115. A. C. Wilson, "American Indian History or Non-Indian Perceptions of American Indian History?," *American Indian Quarterly* 20, no. 1 (1996): 3–5; Swisher, "Why Indian People Should Be the Ones to Write about Indian Education."

116. Meness, "Smoke Signals as Equipment for Living"; Wilson, "American Indian History."

117. Meness, "Smoke Signals as Equipment for Living."

118. Fixico, "Ethics and Responsibilities in Writing American Indian History."

119. Mihesuah, *American Indians*.

120. Fixico, "Ethics and Responsibilities in Writing American Indian History"; Wilson, "American Indian History."

121. Sanchez, "Buying into Racism"; Keever, Martindale, and Weston, *U.S. News Coverage of Racial Minorities*.

122. Watson, "The Future Is Our Past," 12; Keever, Martindale, and Weston, *U.S. News Coverage of Racial Minorities*.

123. "U.S.-Dakota War of 1862," Minnesota History Center," http://libguides.mnhs.org/war1862.

124. M. Trahant, "It's Time to Change the Story about Indian Health," *Health News & Notes* April 2011, http://www.npaihb.org.

125. M. Trahant, "The Data May Be a Mess, but Can It Still Be Useful to Indian Country?," Enduring Legacies: Native Case Studies, 2011, http://nativecases.evergreen.edu.

126. U.S. Census Bureau, "Shapefiles for Pine Ridge Reservation," 2000, http://www2.census.gov.

127. Jeff Harjo, executive director, Native American Journalists Association, interview with authors, March 16, 2012.

128. E. Cook-Lynn, "American Indian Intellectualism and the New Indian Story," *American Indian Quarterly* 20, no. 1 (1996): 57–76.

129. Wilson, "American Indian History"; Swisher, "Why Indian People Should Be the Ones to Write about Indian Education"; Wilson, Gutiérrez, and Chao, *Racism, Sexism, and the Media*.

130. Swisher, "Why Indian People Should Be the Ones to Write about Indian Education"; Wilson, "American Indian History."

131. Cook-Lynn, "American Indian Intellectualism."
132. Wilson, Gutiérrez, and Chao, *Racism, Sexism, and the Media.*
133. Avila-Hernandez, "Native Americans in the Twenty-First Century Newsroom."
134. C. Hamilton, "Recruiting Native Journalists: The New Storytellers," *Winds of Change* 11, no. 2 (1996): 32–36; McAuliffe, "Elevating Journalism in Indian Country."
135. Freedom Forum, "AIJI Opens with Promise of Changed Lives," 2013, http://freedomforumdiversity.org.
136. McAuliffe, "Elevating Journalism in Indian Country."

Chapter 2. The Data

1. T. R. Lindlof and B. C. Taylor, *Qualitative Communication Research Methods*, 2nd ed. (Los Angeles: Sage, 2002), 171.
2. See appendix.
3. R. D. Wimmer and J. R. Dominick, *Mass Media Research: An Introduction*, 8th ed. (Belmont, CA: Thomas-Wadsworth, 2006), 135.
4. Wimmer and Dominick, *Mass Media Research.*
5. Wimmer and Dominick, *Mass Media Research.*
6. Wimmer and Dominick, *Mass Media Research*, 99.
7. Bryan Pollard, executive editor, *Cherokee Phoenix*, interview with authors, February 14, 2012.
8. Marley Shebala, senior reporter, *Navajo Times*, interview with authors, June 2012.
9. Mark Trahant, journalist, *Trahant Reports*, interview with authors, April 10, 2012.
10. Peggy Berryhill, president/general manager, KGUA, interview with authors, January 3, 2012.
11. Shondiin Silversmith, intern, *Navajo Times*, interview with authors, June 2012.
12. Tom Arviso, executive officer and publisher, *Navajo Times*, interview with authors, June 2012.
13. Will Kie, associate producer, *Native America Calling*, interview with authors, June 2012.
14. Jeanie Greene, reporter/anchor, *Heartbeat Alaska*, interview with authors, December 7, 2012.
15. Arviso, interview, June 2012.
16. Lindlof and Taylor, *Qualitative Communication Research.*
17. Lindlof and Taylor, *Qualitative Communication Research*, 147.
18. Lindlof and Taylor, *Qualitative Communication Research.*
19. Lindlof and Taylor, *Qualitative Communication Research.*
20. J. B. Singer, "Ethnography," *Journalism & Mass Communication Quarterly* 86, no. 1 (2009):

191–98.

21. *Navajo Times*, http://navajotimes.com/.

22. Tom Arviso, executive officer and publisher, *Navajo Times*, interview with authors, February 14, 2012.

23. "Navajo Nation Code Annotated," Navajo Nation, 2009, epub.sub.uni-hamburg.de/epub/volltexte/2009/1893/pdf/nnca.pdf, 2.

24. Arviso, interview, February 14, 2012.

25. Marley Shebala, "Covering Business on Tribals Lands," Daylong session, July 13, 2011, Donald W. Reynolds National Center for Business Journalism.

26. Koahnic Broadcast Corporation, http://koahnicbroadcast.org.

27. Burt Poley, network manager, NV1, interview with authors, December 28, 2011.

28. Will Kie, associate producer, *Native America Calling*, interview with authors, May 16, 2013.

29. Joaqlin Estus, news director, KNBA, interview with authors, June 18, 2013.

30. Native Voice One, http://www.nv1.org/.

31. Paul DeMain, executive director and publisher, Indian Country Communications, interview with authors, July 17, 2012.

32. Paul DeMain, executive director and publisher, Indian Country Communications, interview with authors, July 30, 2012.

33. "Suspected Arson at LCO Reservation, Hayward," *Sawyer County Record*, July 17, 2013, http://www.apg-wi.com/sawyer_county_record/.

34. Paul DeMain, executive director and publisher, Indian Country Communications, interview with authors, February 3, 2012.

Chapter 3. Helping Native Voices Breathe

1. Tom Arviso, executive officer and publisher, *Navajo Times*, interview with authors, June 2012.

2. Arviso, interview, June 2012.

3. Arviso, interview, June 2012.

4. Arviso, interview, June 2012.

5. Franklin Yazzie, human resources manager, *Navajo Times*, interview with authors, June 2012.

6. Leonard Sylvan, press operator, *Navajo Times*, interview with authors, June 2012.

7. D. T. Healy and P. J. Orneski, *Native American Flags* (Norman: University of Oklahoma Press, 2003).

8. Paul Natonabah, head photographer, *Navajo Times*, interview with authors, June 2012.

9. Natonabah, interview, June 2012.

10. Arviso, interview, June 2012.

11. Arviso, interview, June 2012.

12. Arviso, interview, June 2012; Marley Shebala, senior reporter, *Navajo Times*, interview with authors, June 2012.

13. Arviso, interview, June 2012.

14. Arviso, interview, June 2012.

15. Arviso, interview, June 2012.

16. Tom Arviso, executive officer and publisher, *Navajo Times*, interview with authors, June 18, 2013.

17. Arviso, interview, June 2012.

18. Arviso, interview, June 2012.

19. Arviso, interview, June 2012.

20. Arviso, interview, June 2012; Shebala, interview, June 2012.

21. Shebala, interview, June 2012.

22. Native Voice One, http://www.nv1.org.

23. Loren Dixon, program director, KNBA, interview with authors, May 29, 2013.

24. *Heartbeat Alaska*, http://tunein.com/radio/Heartbeat-Alaska-p53393/.

25. Jeanie Greene, reporter/anchor, *Heartbeat Alaska*, interview with authors, June 6, 2013.

26. Greene, interview, June 6, 2013.

27. Peggy Berryhill, president/general manager, KGUA, interview with authors, June 5, 2013.

28. KGUA, http://www.kgua.org/.

29. Berryhill, interview, June 5, 2013.

30. Berryhill, interview, June 5, 2013.

31. KIDE, http://www.kidefm.org.

32. Joseph Orozco, station manager, KIDE, interview with authors, May 1, 2012.

33. Paul DeMain, executive director and publisher, Indian Country Communications, interview with authors, February 3, 2012.

34. DeMain, interview, February 3, 2012.

35. Bryan Pollard, executive editor, *Cherokee Phoenix*, interview with authors, February 14, 2012.

36. Bryan Pollard, executive editor, *Cherokee Phoenix*, interview with authors, June 8, 2013.

37. Vision Maker Media (formerly Native American Public Telecommunications, Inc.), http://www.visionmakermedia.org; Shirley Kay Sneve, executive director, Vision Maker Media, interview with authors, May 15, 2013.

38. Shirley Kay Sneve, executive director, Vision Maker Media, interview with authors, June 5, 2013.

39. *Trahant Reports*, http://www.trahantreports.com.

40. Ruth Hopkins, founding writer, Last Real Indians, interview with authors, June 18, 2013; Last Real Indians, http://lastrealindians.com.

41. Ruth Hopkins, founding writer, Last Real Indians, interview with authors, May 30, 2013.

42. Chase Iron Eyes, creator, Last Real Indians, interview with authors, January 13, 2012.

43. Arviso, interview, June 2012.

44. Arviso, interview, June 2012.

45. Shebala, interview, June 2012.

46. Shebala, interview, June 2012.

47. Shebala, interview, June 2012.

48. Yazzie, interview, June 2012.

49. Arviso, interview, June 2012.

50. Arviso, interview, June 2012.

51. Bill Donovan, freelance reporter, *Navajo Times*, interview with authors, June 2012.

52. Donovan, interview, June 2012.

53. J. Meness, "Smoke Signals as Equipment for Living," in *American Indians and the Mass Media*, ed. M. G. Carstarphen and J. P. Sanchez (Norman: University of Oklahoma Press, 2012), 94–112.

54. Donovan, interview, June 2012.

55. Orozco, interview, May 1, 2012.

56. Shebala, interview, June 2012.

57. Shebala, interview, June 2012.

58. Yazzie, interview, June 2012; Sylvan, interview, June 2012.

59. Arviso, interview, June 2012.

60. Shebala, interview, June 2012.

61. Yazzie, interview, June 2012.

62. Bobby Martin, production manager, *Navajo Times*, interview with authors, June 2012.

63. E. Guskin and A. Mitchell, "Innovating News in Native Communities," *The State of the News Media 2012*, Pew Research Center Project for Excellence in Journalism, http://stateofthemedia.org.

64. Pollard, interview, February 14, 2012.

65. G. Doyle, "From Television to Multi-Platform: Less from More or More for Less?," *Convergence* 16, no. 4 (2010): 431–49.

66. T. Williams, "Quietly, Indians Reshape Cities and Reservations," *New York Times*, April 13, 2013, http://www.nytimes.com.

67. Guskin and Mitchell, "Innovating News in Native Communities."

68. Yazzie, interview, June 2012.

69. Will Kie, associate producer, *Native America Calling*, interview with authors, June 2012.

70. Kie, interview, June 2012.

71. Joaqlin Estus, news director, KNBA, interview with authors, July 17, 2012. Due to budget cuts, KNBA in February 2016 dropped its APRN membership. Estus still shares her stories with other stations and uses theirs.

72. Estus, interview, July 17, 2012.

73. Estus, interview, July 17, 2012.

74. Jeff Harjo, executive director, Native American Journalists Association, interview with authors, March 16, 2012.

75. Arviso, interview, June 2012.

76. Noel Lyn Smith, reporter, *Navajo Times*, interview with authors, June 2012.

77. Rebecca Landsberry, membership and communications manager, Native American Journalists Association, interview with authors, April 17, 2013.

78. Landsberry, interview, April 17, 2013.

79. Arviso, interview, June 2012.

80. R. Boney, "Cherokeespace.com: Native Social Networking," in Carstarphen and Sanchez, *American Indians and the Mass Media*, 222–26.

81. Smith, interview, June 2012.

82. Smith, interview, June 2012.

83. Williams, "Quietly, Indians Reshape Cities and Reservations"; Guskin and Mitchell, "Innovating News in Native Communities."

84. J. Harjo, interview, March 16, 2012; Elise Bennett, graphic designer, *Navajo Times*, interview with authors, June 2012; Quentin Jodie, sports reporter, *Navajo Times*, interview with authors, June 2012.

85. Noel Lyn Smith, reporter, *Navajo Times*, interview with authors, June 26, 2013; Duane Beyal, editor, *Navajo Times*, interview with authors, June 2012.

86. Kie, interview, June 2012.

87. Native American Journalists Association, http://www.naja.com; Arviso, interview, June 2012.

88. Arviso, interview, June 2012.

89. Pollard, interview, February 14, 2012.

90. DeMain, interview, February 3, 2012.

91. J. A. Avila-Hernandez, "Native Americans in the Twenty-First Century Newsroom: Breaking through Barriers in New Media," in Carstarphen and Sanchez, *American Indians and the Mass Media*, 227–31.

92. Mark Trahant, journalist, *Trahant Reports*, interview with authors, April 10, 2012.

93. Trahant, interview, April 10, 2012.

94. "How Did Native Americans Impact the 2012 Election?" Vison Maker Media, http://www.visionmakermedia.org/watch/how-did-native-americans-impact-2012-election.

95. Trahant, interview, April 10, 2012.

96. Associated Press, "B-52 Crashes on Navajo Lands," *New York Times*, October 17, 1984, http://www.nytimes.com.

97. Natonabah, interview, June 2012.

98. Natonabah, interview, June 2012.

99. Natonabah, interview, June 2012.

100. Natonabah, interview, June 2012.

101. Shebala, interview, June 2012.

102. Shebala, interview, June 2012.

103. Josh Pearson, web producer/editor, Indian Country Communications, interview with authors, August 12, 2012.

Chapter 4. Looking Forward

1. Peggy Berryhill, president/general manager, KGUA, interview with authors, January 3, 2012; Shirley Kay Sneve, executive director, Vision Maker Media, interview with authors, January 3, 2012; Bryan Pollard, executive editor, *Cherokee Phoenix*, interview with authors, February 14, 2012.

2. Pollard, interview, February 14, 2012.

3. Berryhill, interview, January 3, 2012; Pollard, interview, February 14, 2012.

4. Marley Shebala, senior reporter, *Navajo Times*, interview with authors, June 2012; Berryhill, interview, January 3, 2012; Sneve, interview, January 3, 2012; Pollard, interview, February 14, 2012.

5. Jeanie Greene, reporter/anchor, *Heartbeat Alaska*, interview with authors, December 7, 2012.

6. Antonia Gonzales, anchor/producer, *National Native News*, interview with authors, October 10, 2012.

7. Will Kie, associate producer, *Native America Calling*, interview with authors, June 2012.

8. Berryhill, interview, January 3, 2012.

9. Chase Iron Eyes, creator, Last Real Indians, interview with authors, January 13, 2012.

10. Jeff Harjo, executive director, Native American Journalists Association, interview with authors, March 16, 2012.

11. Shebala, interview, June 2012.

12. Shebala, interview, June 2012.

13. Iron Eyes, interview, January 13, 2012.

14. Kie, interview, June 2012.

15. Pollard, interview, February 14, 2012.

16. C. C. Wilson, F. Gutiérrez, and L. M. Chao, *Racism, Sexism, and the Media: Multicultural Issues into the New Communications Age*, 4th ed. (Los Angeles: Sage, 2013); E. Guskin and A. Mitchell "Innovating News in Native Communities" *The State of the News Media 2012*, Pew Research Center Project for Excellence in Journalism, http://stateofthemedia.org.

17. Wilson, Gutiérrez, and Chao, *Racism, Sexism, and the Media*.

18. Paul DeMain, executive director and publisher, Indian Country Communications, interview with authors, February 3, 2012.

19. DeMain, interview, February 3, 2012.

20. Berryhill, interview, January 3, 2012.

21. Native Media Resource Center, http://nativemediaresourcecenter.org.

22. KGUA, http://www.kgua.org.

23. Patty Talahongva, independent producer, interview with authors, January 4, 2012.

24. Talahongva, interview, January 4, 2012.

25. DeMain, interview, February 3, 2012.

26. DeMain, interview, February 3, 2012.

27. Joseph Orozco, station manager, KIDE, interview with authors, May 1, 2012.

28. Orozco, interview, May 1, 2012.

29. Shebala, interview, June 2012.

30. Shebala, interview, June 2012.

31. Shebala, interview, June 2012.

32. Shebala, interview, June 2012.

33. Greene, interview, December 7, 2012.

34. Shebala, interview, June 2012.

35. Shebala, interview, June 2012.

36. Pollard, interview, February 14, 2012.

37. Tom Arviso, executive officer and publisher, *Navajo Times*, interview with authors, June 2012.

38. Arviso, interview, June 2012.

Chapter 5. Digital Visibility

1. M. Prior, *Post-Broadcast Democracy: How Media Choice Increases Inequality in Political Involvement and Polarizes Elections* (Cambridge: Cambridge University Press, 2007).

2. B. Duncan, *Living Stories of the Cherokee* (Chapel Hill: University of North Carolina Press, 1998).

3. Tom Arviso, executive officer and publisher, *Navajo Times*, interview with authors, June 2012.

4. Bureau of Indian Affairs, U.S. Department of the Interior, http://www.indianaffairs.gov.

5. Duncan, *Living Stories of the Cherokee.*

6. C. C. Wilson, F. Gutiérrez, and L. M. Chao, *Racism, Sexism, and the Media: Multicultural Issues into the New Communications Age*, 4th ed. (Los Angeles: Sage, 2013).

7. N7 Fund, http://n7fund.com/.

8. Q. Jodie, "Schimmel Sisters Savoring the Spotlight," *Navajo Times*, April 18, 2013, http://www.navajotimes.com.

9. "Shoni Schimmel Native Woman Basketball Star, Community Page Leadership," https://www.facebook.com/pages/Shoni-Schimmel-Woman-Native-American-Basketball-star/323761140982325?fref=ts.

10. A. Minard, "Rez Ball Is Big Time in the Navajo Nation," Indian Country Today Media Network, May 18, 2013, http://indiancountrytodaymedianetwork.com.

11. "Shoni Schimmel Native Woman Basketball Star, Community Page Leadership."

12. Jodie, "Schimmel Sisters Savoring the Spotlight."

13. Jodie, "Schimmel Sisters Savoring the Spotlight."

14. Associated Press, "Oregonians Shoni and Jude Schimmel Showcase 'Rez Ball' at Louisville," *The Oregonian*, April 8, 2013, http://www.oregonlive.com.

15. Associated Press, "Oregonians Shoni and Jude Schimmel Showcase 'Rez Ball.'"

16. ICTMN Staff, "Native Language App Gets Cool Reception," Indian Country Today Media Network, February 22, 2012, http://indiancountrytodaymedianetwork.com.

17. J. Murphy, "Technology Specialists Help Advance Cherokee Language," *Cherokee Phoenix*, March 11, 2013, http://www.cherokeephoenix.org; R. Boney, "Cherokeespace.com: Native Social Networking," in *American Indians and the Mass Media*, ed. M. G. Carstarphen and J. P. Sanchez (Norman: University of Oklahoma Press, 2012), 222–26.

18. Indian Country TV, http://indiancountrytv.com.

19. R. Chavez, "Joining the Circle: A Yakima Story," in Carstarphen and Sanchez, *American Indians and the Mass Media*, 232–34.

20. E. Guskin and A. Mitchell, "Innovating News in Native Communities," *The State of the News Media 2012*, Pew Research Center Project for Excellence in Journalism, http://stateofthemedia.org.

21. Jeff Harjo, executive director, Native American Journalists Association, interview with authors, March 16, 2012; Noel Lyn Smith, reporter, *Navajo Times*, interview with authors,

June 2012.

22. Bryan Pollard, executive editor, *Cherokee Phoenix*, interview with authors, February 14, 2012.

23. U.S. Census Bureau, "American Indians by the Numbers," Infoplease, 2012, http://www.infoplease.com.

References

Allan, S., and B. Zelizer. "Rules of Engagement: Journalism and War." In *Reporting War: Journalism in Wartime*, ed. S. Allan and B. Zelizer, 3–21. New York: Routledge, 2004.

Allen, J. "Ethnic Media Reaching Record Numbers in U.S." CommonDreams. June 6, 2009. Http://www.commondreams.org.

Anderson, C. G. "American Indian Tribal Web Sites: A Review and Comparison." *Electronic Library* 21, no. 5 (2003): 450–55.

Associated Press. "B-52 Crashes on Navajo Lands." *New York Times*. October 17, 1984. Http://www.nytimes.com/1984/10/17/us/b-52-crashes-on-navajo-lands.html.

———. "Oregonians Shoni and Jude Schimmel Showcase 'Rez Ball' at Louisville." *The Oregonian*. April 8, 2013. Http://www.oregonlive.com/collegebasketball/index.ssf/2013/04/oregonians_shoni_and_jude_schi.html.

Aufderheide, P. "Big Media and Little Media: The Journalistic Informal Sector during the Invasion of Iraq." In *Reporting War: Journalism in Wartime*, ed. S. Allan and B. Zelizer, 333–46 New York: Routledge, 2004.

Avila-Hernandez, J. A. "Native Americans in the Twenty-First Century Newsroom: Breaking through Barriers in New Media." In *American Indians and the Mass Media*, ed. M. G. Carstarphen and J. P. Sanchez, 227–31. Norman: University of Oklahoma Press, 2012.

Ben-Porath, E. N., and L. K. Shaker. "News Images, Race, and Attribution in the Wake of

Hurricane Katrina." *Journal of Communication* 60, no. 3 (2010): 466–90.

Bennett, W. L. "Toward a Theory of Press–State Relations in the United States." *Journal of Communication* 40, no. 2 (1990): 103–27.

Berkowitz, D. *Social Meanings of News: A Text-Reader*. Los Angeles: Sage, 1997.

———, ed. *Cultural Meanings of News: A Text-Reader*. Los Angeles: Sage, 2010.

Blumler, J. G., and M. Gurevitch. "Politicians and the Press: An Essay on Role Relationships." In *Handbook of Political Communication*, ed. D. D. Nimmo and K. R. Sanders, 467–93. Beverly Hills: Sage, 1981.

Boney, R. "Cherokeespace.com: Native Social Networking." In *American Indians and the Mass Media*, ed. M. G. Carstarphen and J. P. Sanchez, 222–26. Norman: University of Oklahoma Press, 2012.

Bureau of Indian Affairs. "What We Do." U.S. Department of the Interior. Http://www.bia.gov/WhatWeDo/.

Campbell, C. P. *Race and News: Critical Perspectives*. New York: Routledge, 2012.

Carey, J. "A Cultural Approach to Communication." In *Communication as Culture: Essays on Media and Society*, 13–36. New York: Routledge, 1992.

Chavez, R. "Joining the Circle: A Yakima Story." In *American Indians and the Mass Media*, ed. M. G. Carstarphen and J. P. Sanchez, 232–34. Norman: University of Oklahoma Press, 2012.

Cook, T. E. "Afterword: Political Values and Production Values." *Political Communication* 13 (1996): 469–81.

———. *Governing with the News*. Chicago, IL: University of Chicago Press, 2005.

Cook-Lynn, E. "American Indian Intellectualism and the New Indian Story." *American Indian Quarterly* 20, no. 1 (1996): 57–76.

Daniels, G. L. "The Role of Native American Print and Online Media in the 'Era of Big Stories': A Comparative Case Study of Native American Outlets' Coverage of the Red Lake Shootings." *Journalism* 7, no. 3 (2006): 321–42.

Dates, J. L., and W. Barlow. *Split Image: African Americans in the Mass Media*. 2nd ed. Washington, DC: Howard University Press, 1993.

Dixon, T. L. "Crime News and Racialized Beliefs: Understanding the Relationship between Local News Viewing and Perceptions of African Americans and Crime." *Journal of Communication* 58, no. 1 (2008): 106–25.

Dixon, T. L., and D. Linz. "Race and the Misrepresentation of Victimization on Local Television News." *Communication Research* 27, no. 5 (2000): 547–73.

Doyle, G. "From Television to Multi-Platform: Less from More or More for Less?" *Convergence* 16, no. 4 (2010): 431–49.

Dunaway, J. "Markets, Ownership, and the Quality of Campaign News Coverage." *Journal of*

Politics 70, no. 4 (2008): 1193–202.

Duncan, B. *Living Stories of the Cherokee*. Chapel Hill: University of North Carolina Press, 1998.

Eliasoph, N. "Routines and the Making of Oppositional News." *Critical Studies in Mass Communication* 5 (1988): 313–34.

Entman, R. M. "Framing: Toward Clarification of a Fractured Paradigm." *Journal of Communication* 43, no. 4 (1993): 51–58.

———. "Representation and Reality in the Portrayal of Black on Network Television News." *Journalism & Mass Communication Quarterly* 71, no. 3 (1994): 509–20.

Entman, R., and A. Rojecki. *The Black Image in the White Mind: Media and Race in America.* Chicago: University of Chicago Press, 2001.

Ettema, J. S. "Crafting Cultural Resonance: Imaginative Power in Everyday Journalism." *Journalism* 6, no. 2 (2005): 131–52.

Feldman, L. "The News about Comedy Young Audiences: *The Daily Show*, and Evolving Notions of Journalism." *Journalism* 8, no. 4 (2007): 406–27.

Fiske, S. T., A. J. C. Cuddy, and P. Glick. "Universal Dimensions of Social Cognition: Warmth and Competence." *Trends in Cognitive Sciences* 11, no. 2 (2007): 77–83.

Fixico, D. L. "Ethics and Responsibilities in Writing American Indian History." *American Indian Quarterly* 20, no. 1 (1996): 29–39.

Freedom Forum. "AIJI Opens with Promise of Changed Lives." June 20, 2013. Http://freedomforumdiversity.org/tag/journalism/.

Gerbner, G., L. Gross, N. Signorielli, and M. Morgan. "Television Violence, Victimization, and Power." *American Behavioral Scientist* 23, no. 5 (1980): 705–16.

Grabe, M. E., and E. P. Bucy. *Image Bite Politics: News and the Visual Framing of Elections.* Oxford: Oxford University Press, 2009.

Grinberg, E. "Native American Designers Fight Cultural Caricatures." CNN. November 30, 2012. Http://www.cnn.com/2012/11/30/living/native-american-fashion-appropriation.

Gross, D. "Twitter User Unknowingly Reported bin Laden Attack." CNN. May 2, 2011. Http://www.cnn.com/2011/TECH/social.media/05/02/osama.twitter.reports/index.html.

Grossman, L. "Iran Protests: Twitter, the Medium of the Movement." *TIME*. June 17, 2009. Http://www.time.com/time/world/article/0,8599,1905125,00.html.

Guskin, E., and A. Mitchell. "Innovating News in Native Communities" *The State of the News Media 2012*. Pew Research Center Project for Excellence in Journalism. Http://stateofthemedia.org/2012/native-american-news-media/.

Hall, S. "The Rediscovery of 'Ideology': Return of the Repressed in Media Studies." In *Culture, Society and the Media*, ed. M. Gurevitch, J. Curran, T. Bennett, and J. Wollacott, 111–41. London: Methuen, 1982.

———. "The White of Their Eyes: Racist Ideologies and the Media." In *Gender, Race, and Class in Media: A Text-Reader*, ed. G. Dines and J. M. Humez, 271–82. Los Angeles: Sage, 1995.

Hamilton, C. "Recruiting Native Journalists: The New Storytellers." *Winds of Change* 11, no. 2 (1996): 32–36.

Hamilton, J. T. *All the News That's Fit to Sell: How the Market Transforms Information into News.* Princeton, NJ: Princeton University Press, 2004.

Hanks, L. J. *The Struggle for Black Political Empowerment in Three Georgia Counties.* Knoxville: University of Tennessee Press, 1987.

Healy, D. T., and P. J. Orenski. *Native American Flags.* Norman: University of Oklahoma Press, 2003.

ICTMN Staff. "Broadband in Indian Country to Expand." Indian Country Today Media Network. March 3, 2011. Http://indiancountrytodaymedianetwork.com/article/broadband-in-indian-country-to-expand-21008.

———. "Native Language App Gets Cool Reception." Indian Country Today Media Network. February 22, 2012. Http://indiancountrytodaymedianetwork.com/2012/02/22/native-language-app-gets-cool-reception-99211.

———. "Suzan Harjo to Receive Presidential Medal of Freedom." Indian Country Today Media Network. November 11, 2014. Http://indiancountrytodaymedianetwork.com/2014/11/11/suzan-harjo-receive-presidential-medal-freedom-157791.

Indianz.com. "President Barack Obama Wins a Second Term in the White House." November 7, 2012. Http://www.indianz.com/News/2012/007642.asp?print=1.

Izard, R. S. *Diversity That Works.* Baton Rouge: Louisiana State University Press, 2008.

Jha, S., and R. S. Izard. "Who Got to Talk about It: Sourcing and Attribution in Broadcast News Coverage of the First 24 Hours of the 9/11 Tragedy." *Seattle Journal for Social Justice* 4, no. 1 (2005): 101–18.

Jodie, Q. "Schimmel Sisters Savoring the Spotlight." *Navajo Times.* April 18, 2013. Http://www.navajotimes.com/sports/2013/0413/041813sch.php.

Kahle, S., N. Yu, and E. Whiteside. "Another Disaster: An Examination of Portrayals of Race in Hurricane Katrina Coverage." *Visual Communications Quarterly* 14, no. 2 (2007): 75–89.

Keever, B. A. D., C. Martindale, and M. A. Weston, eds. *U.S. News Coverage of Racial Minorities: A Sourcebook, 1934–1996.* Westport, CT: Greenwood Press, 1997.

Kemper, K. R. "Who Speaks for Indigenous Peoples? Tribal Journalists, Rhetorical Sovereignty, and Freedom of Expression." *Journalism & Communication Monographs* 12, no. 1 (2010): 3–58.

Kopacz, M., and B. L. Lawton. "The YouTube Indian: Portrayals of Native Americans on a Viral Video Site." *New Media & Society* 13, no. 2 (2011): 330–49.

Krosgstad, J. M. "Social Media Preferences Vary by Race and Ethnicity." Pew Research Center. February 3, 2015. Http://www.pewresearch.org/fact-tank/2015/02/03/social-media-preferences-vary-by-race-and-ethnicity/.

Kurpius, D. D. "Sources and Civic Journalism: Changing Patterns of Reporting?" *Journalism & Mass Communication Quarterly* 79, no. 4 (2002): 853–66.

Lieber, L. D. "Capitalizing on Demographic Change: How Your Organization Can Prepare for the Global Workplace." DiversityBusiness.com. 2013. Http://www.diversitybusiness.com/news/diversity.magazine/99200841.asp.

Lindlof, T. R., and B. C. Taylor. *Qualitative Communication Research Methods.* 2nd ed. Los Angeles: Sage, 2002.

Lippmann, W. *Public Opinion.* New York: Harcourt, Brace and Co., 1922.

Lule, J. *Daily News, Eternal Stories: The Mythological Role of Journalism.* New York: Guilford Press, 2001.

McAuliffe, D., Jr. "Elevating Journalism in Indian Country." American Society of Newspaper Editors. 2000. Http://files.asne.org/kiosk/editor/00.aug/mcauliffe1.htm.

McDonnell-Smith, M. "Asians Are Fastest-Growing U.S. Ethnic Group, Blacks Are Slowest, Reports U.S. Census Bureau." Diversity Inc. June 17, 2013. Http://www.diversityinc.com/diversity-and-inclusion/asians-are-fastest-growing-u-s-ethnic-group-in-2012-blacks-are-slowest-reports-u-s-census-bureau/.

McManus, J. H. *Market-Driven Journalism: Let the Citizen Beware?* Los Angeles: Sage, 1994.

Mendelberg, T. "A Theory of Racial Appeals." In *The Race Card: Campaign Strategy, Implicit Messages, and the Norm of Equality*, 3–27. Princeton, NJ: Princeton University Press, 2001.

Meness, J. "Smoke Signals as Equipment for Living." In *American Indians and the Mass Media*, ed. M. G. Carstarphen and J. P. Sanchez, 94–112. Norman: University of Oklahoma Press, 2012.

Merina, V. "The Internet: Continuing the Legacy of Storytelling." *Nieman Reports*, fall 2005, 32–34.

Merskin, D. "Winnebagos, Cherokees, Apaches and Dakotas: The Persistence of Stereotyping of American Indians in American Advertising Brands." *Howard Journal of Communications* 12 (2001): 159–69.

Mihesuah, D. A. *American Indians: Stereotypes and Realities.* Atlanta: Clarity, 1996.

Miller, A., and V. Bemker LaPoe. "Sourcing in National vs. Local Television News Coverage of the Deepwater Horizon Oil Spill: A Study of Experts, Victims, Roles and Race." Paper presented at Association for Education in Journalism and Mass Communication, St. Louis, MO, August 2011.

Miller, A., and S. Roberts. "Visual Agenda-Setting & Proximity after Hurricane Katrina: A Study of Those Closest to the Event." *Visual Communication Quarterly* 17, no. 1 (2010): 31–46.

Minard, A. "Rez Ball Is Big Time in the Navajo Nation." Indian Country Today Media Network. May 18, 2013. Http://indiancountrytodaymedianetwork.com/2013/05/18/rez-ball-big-time-navajo-nation-149383.

Minnesota History Center. "U.S.-Dakota War of 1862." Http://libguides.mnhs.org/war1862.

Mitten, L. "Indians on the Internet—Selected Native American Web Sites." *Electronic Library* 21, no. 5 (2003): 443–49.

Molotch, H., and M. Lester. "News as Purposive Behavior: On the Strategic Use of Routine Events, Accidents, and Scandals." *American Sociological Review* 39 (1974): 101–12.

Mossberger, K., C. J. Tolbert, and M. C. Stansbury. *Virtual Inequality: Beyond the Digital Divide.* Washington, DC: Georgetown University Press, 2003.

Moya-Smith, S. "New Anti-Redskins Video Says FedEx 'Embraces Racism.'" Indian Country Today Media Network. September 4, 2014. Http://indiancountrytodaymedianetwork.com/2014/09/04/new-anti-redskins-video-says-fedex-embraces-racism-156746.

Murphy, J. "Technology Specialists Help Advance Cherokee Language." *Cherokee Phoenix.* March 11, 2013. Http://www.cherokeephoenix.org/Article/Index/7082.

Page, B. I. "The Mass Media as Political Actors." *PS: Political Science and Politics* 29, no. 1 (1996): 20–24.

Petill, C. "'Victoria's Secret Fashion Show' Leads CBS for the Night." *Examiner.* December 6, 2012. Http://www.examiner.com/article/victoria-s-secret-fashion-show-leads-cbs-for-the-night.

Phillips, S. G. "'Indians on Our Warpath': World War II Images of Native Americans in *Life* Magazine, 1937–1949." In *American Indians and the Mass Media,* ed. M. G. Carstarphen and J. P. Sanchez, 33–55. Norman: University of Oklahoma Press, 2012.

Piller, I. "Passing for a Native Speaker: Identity and Success in Second Language Learning." *Journal of Sociolinguistics* 6, no. 2 (2002): 179–208.

Poindexter, P. M., L. Smith, and D. Heider. "Race and Ethnicity in Local Television News: Framing, Story Assignments, and Source Selections." *Journal of Broadcasting & Electronic Media* 47, no. 4 (2003): 524–36.

Pond Cummings, A. D. "A Shifting Wind? Media Stereotyping of American Indians and the Law." In *American Indians and the Mass Media,* ed. M. G. Carstarphen and J. P. Sanchez, 185–212. Norman: University of Oklahoma Press, 2012.

Postman, N. *Amusing Ourselves to Death: Public Discourse in the Age of Show Business.* New York: Penguin, 2006.

Prior, M. *Post-Broadcast Democracy: How Media Choice Increases Inequality in Political Involvement and Polarizes Elections.* Cambridge: Cambridge University Press, 2007.

Reeves, K. *Voting Hopes or Fears? White Voters, Black Candidates and Racial Politics in America.* Oxford: Oxford University Press, 1997.

Roy, L., and D. Raitt. "The Impact of IT on Indigenous Peoples." *Electronic Library* 21, no. 5 (2003): 411–13.

Sakaki, T., M. Okazaki, and Y. Matsuo. "Earthquake Shakes Twitter Users: Real-time Event Detection by Social Sensors." Unpublished paper presented at the International World Wide Web Conference, Raleigh, NC, April 2010.

Sanchez, V. "Buying into Racism: American Indian Product Icons in the American Marketplace." In *American Indians and the Mass Media*, ed. M. G. Carstarphen and J. P. Sanchez, 153–69. Norman: University of Oklahoma Press, 2012.

Sawyer County Record. "Suspected Arson at LCO Reservation, Hayward." July 17, 2012. Http://www.apg-wi.com/sawyer_county_record/multimedia/photos/suspected-arson-at-lco-reservation-hayward/youtube_055165b7-a8e3–50b5-a860–128a3dc3af34.html.

Schilling, V. "The Revenant's Elk Dog: A Conversation with Duane Howard." Indian Country Today Media Network. February 4, 2016. Http://indiancountrytodaymedianetwork.com/2016/02/04/revenants-elk-dog-conversation-duane-howard-163295.

Schwarz, H. "Colorado Theater Shooting Witnesses Take to Twitter and Reddit to Share Their Stories." Media-ite. July 20, 2012. Http://www.mediaite.com/online/colorado-theater-shooting-witnesses-take-to-twitter-and-reddit-to-share-their-stories/.

Seymour, R. "Names, not Nations: Patterned References to Indigenous Americans in the *New York Times* and *Los Angeles Times*, 1999–2000." In *American Indians and the Mass Media*, ed. M. G. Carstarphen and J. P. Sanchez, 73–93. Norman: University of Oklahoma Press, 2012.

Shebala, Marley. "Covering Business on Tribals Lands." Daylong session, July 13, 2011. Donald W. Reynolds National Center for Business Journalism.

Shoemaker, N. *Clearing a Path: Theorizing the Past in Native American Studies.* New York: Routledge, 2002.

Shoemaker, P. J., and S. D. Reese. *Mediating the Message: Theories of Influences on Mass Media Content.* 2nd ed. White Plains, NY: Longman, 1996.

Singer, J. B. "The Metro Wide Web: Changes in Newspapers' Gatekeeping Role Online." *Journalism & Mass Communication Quarterly* 78, no. 1 (2001): 65–80.

———. "Strange Bedfellows? The Diffusion of Convergence in Four News Organizations." *Journalism Studies* 5, no. 1 (2004): 3–18.

———. "Ethnography." *Journalism & Mass Communication Quarterly* 86, no. 1 (2009): 191–98.

Sloan, W. D. *The Media in America: A History.* 8th ed. Northrop, AL: Vision Press, 2011.

Srinivasan, R. "Indigenous, Ethnic and Cultural Articulations of New Media." *International*

Journal of Cultural Studies 9, no. 4 (2006): 497–518.

Swain, C. M. *Black Faces, Black Interests: The Representation of African Americans in Congress.* Lanham, MD: University Press of America, 2006.

Swisher, K. G. "Why Indian People Should Be the Ones to Write about Indian Education." *American Indian Quarterly* 20, no. 1 (1996): 83–90.

Trahant, M. N. *Pictures of Our Nobler Selves.* Nashville: Freedom Forum First Amendment Center, 1995.

———. "The Data May Be a Mess, but Can It Still Be Useful to Indian Country?" Enduring Legacies: Native Case Studies. 2011. Http://nativecases.evergreen.edu/collection/cases/data-may-be-a-mess.html.

———. "It's Time to Change the Story about Indian Health." *Health News and Notes.* April 2011. Http://www.npaihb.org/images/resources_docs/quarterlynewsletters/2011/april%2004.pdf.

Tuchman, G. *Making News: A Study in the Construction of Reality.* New York: The Free Press, 1978.

University of Pennsylvania. "*Cherokee Phoenix.*" The Online Books Page. Http://onlinebooks.library.upenn.edu/webbin/serial?id=cherokeephoenix.

U.S. Census Bureau. "Shapefiles for Pine Ridge Reservation," 2000. Http://www2.census.gov/cgi-bin/shapefiles/aia-files?aia=2810.

———. "American Indians by the Numbers." Infoplease. 2012. Http://www.infoplease.com/spot/aihmcensus1.html.

Warren, C. "Colorado Theater Shooting: How It Played out Online." Mashable. July 20, 2012. Http://mashable.com/2012/07/20/colorado-theater-shooting-timeline/.

Watson, I. "The Future Is Our Past: We Once Were Sovereign and We Still Are." *Indigenous Law Bulletin* 8, no. 3 (2012): 12–15.

Williams, T. "Quietly, Indians Reshape Cities and Reservations." *New York Times.* April 13, 2013. Http://www.nytimes.com/2013/04/14/us/as-american-indians-move-to-cities-old-and-new-challenges-follow.html.

Wilson, A. C. "American Indian History or Non-Indian Perceptions of American Indian History?" *American Indian Quarterly* 20, no. 1 (1996): 3–5.

Wilson, C. C., F. Gutiérrez, and L. M. Chao. *Racism, Sexism, and the Media: Multicultural Issues into the New Communications Age.* 4th ed. Los Angeles: Sage, 2013.

Wimmer, R. D., and J. R. Dominick. *Mass Media Research: An Introduction.* 8th ed. Belmont, CA: Thomson-Wadsworth, 2006.

Zaller, J. *The Nature and Origins of Mass Opinion.* Cambridge: Cambridge University Press, 1992.

Index

Native journalists by, 2, 29–38, 42–43,
46–52, 57, 68; storytelling theme of, 32,
33, 54, 57; youth/future theme of, 32,
34, 80
Iron Eyes, Chase, 39, 53, 79
Izard, Ralph, 17

J

Jha, S., 17
journalism: advertising in, 7–8, 18, 22–23,
42, 44, 94; audiences, 18; civic, 7, 18, 88;
community, 18; and consumption of
Native news, 64; culture of, 16; DeMain
as leader in, 37–38, 52, 67, 80–82, 93;
diversity in, 39, 78–79; education and,
2, 23–24, 26–27, 81; gender and, 18;
"hierarchy of influence" models and,
16, 17, 21; history's importance to, 85;
interviews of, professionals, 2, 29–38,
42–43, 46–52, 57, 68; longevity in, 84,
85, 96; mass media content and, 16, 18;
Native American, 2, 10, 14, 19, 64, 66,
72, 84–85; Natives in, 23, 25–27, 29, 31;
Native, increases in, 23–24; newsrooms
and, 29; news values in, 16–17; norms
and routines of, 16, 19; offensive attitudes
in, 3, 19; print, 11, 14, 15, 52, 59, 63–67,
72, 84–85; profit in, 5, 18, 22, 36, 42,
49, 89; race and, 18, 19; recruiting and
training youth for, 18, 25–27, 84–86, 96;
sensationalism in, 18; stereotypes and
images in, 3, 4, 19–20
Judd, Paul, 4

K

Karuk Tribe, 52

KGUA (radio), 1, 3, 39, 51, 77, 81
Kickapoo tribe, 78
KIDE (radio): Orozco and, 57, 82; website of,
51–52, 57, 82
Kie, Will, 37, 77
Kiva Club, newspaper of, 83
KNBA (radio), 12, 51; Estus at, 37, 50, 61–63,
114 (n. 71)
Knight Foundation, 31
Koahnic Broadcast Corporation (KBC),
34–37, 49–50, 61, 76–77. *See also* KNBA
(radio); Native Voice One (NV1)
KOB-TV, 69
Kopacz, M., 22
KPFA (radio), 81
Kurpius, D. D., 18
KYAT (radio), 66

L

Lac Courte Oreilles Ojibwe, 38, 52, 93
language, 2, 6, 15, 35, 71; Cherokee, 9, 93;
depth of, 72; descriptive, 58; Hupa,
51; mobile apps for, 92–93; Navajo,
43, 57, 58–59, 66; in newspapers, 52;
radio programming and, 51, 81, 66, 92;
storytelling and, 13–14, 33, 49, 54, 58, 88;
written, 33, 58, 67, 93
Last Real Indians (LRI): blog, 53, 79; website
of, 39, 63
Latinos, 2, 20, 83; diverse media and, 8, 11,
16, 81
LeValdo, Rhonda, 39
Lawton, B. L., 22
Lindlof, T. R., 35
Los Angeles Times, 19
Louisiana State University, 35, 39

M

N

T

U